Strategies for Success

STRATEGIES FOR SUCCESS

Classroom Teaching Techniques
for Students with Learning Differences

Second Edition

Lynn J. Meltzer

Bethany N. Roditi

Joan L. Steinberg

Kathleen Rafter Biddle

Susan E. Taber

Kathleen Boyle Caron

Leta Kniffin

pro·ed
An International Publisher

8700 Shoal Creek Boulevard
Austin, Texas 78757-6897
800/897-3202   Fax 800/397-7633
www.proedinc.com

© 1996, 2006 by PRO-ED, Inc.
8700 Shoal Creek Boulevard
Austin, Texas 78757-6897
800/897-3202   Fax 800/397-7633
www.proedinc.com

Library of Congress Cataloging-in-Publication Data

Strategies for success : classroom teaching techniques for students with learning differences / Lynn J. Meltzer ... [et al.].— 2nd edition.
     p. cm.
   Includes bibliographical references.
   ISBN 1-4164-0065-6 (softcover : alk. paper)
   1. Learning disabled children—Education.   2. Teaching.   I. Meltzer, Lynn.
LC4704.S767 2006
371.9'043—dc22

                                                                2005019463

Art Director: Jason Crosier
Designer: Nancy McKinney-Point

This book is designed in Stone Serif, Univers Condensed, and UniversUltra Condensed.

Printed in the United States of America

1 2 3 4 5 6 7 8 9 10   09 08 07 06 05

Contents

Acknowledgments

We gratefully acknowledge several important people without whom this revision would not have been possible. First, we thank all our colleagues at ResearchILD and the Institute for Learning and Development, whose energy, creativity, intelligence, and dedication inform all of our projects. We are particularly grateful to Donna Kincaid for her invaluable ideas. Second, we want to thank our PRO-ED editor, Beth Donnelly, for her encouragement, patience, and good humor. We also thank two authors of the original *Strategies for Success* book, Michelle Paster and Donna Haynes, as well as Enid Wetzner for her help with the case studies. Finally, we owe tremendous gratitude to all the teachers and students from whom we have learned so much!

I felt I was dumb

Life was worse than glum

Then I was invited to a place called the resource room

That was my doom

Every day I woke up to dread

All mind games in my head

I became so depressed

I could barely get out of bed

But something told me to stay strong

One day, Kira,

You will prove them wrong

So years went by ... there were times all I could do was cry

Frustration galore every day was a bore

In that room struggling to find

If there was anything right about my mind

Then one day, I met someone different

She saw a different me

There was something strange, she used the word we

Feelings of hope, strength surrounded me

I walked out of that room feeling

Free.

—by Kira Repici, 10th grader

Chapter 1

Strategic Learning in the Classroom

I feel like a bottle of ginger ale—I need the fizzle to settle before I can do what I need to do.

—Chris, 5th grader

My mind was like a cloud of gas of different little molecules, speeding around, colliding with each other with no structure. The strategies I learned provided boundaries and parameters to these whizzing dots so that I could make sense of them.

—Brandon, 20 years old

Students such as Chris and Brandon present a special challenge to their parents and teachers because of the inconsistencies in their reasoning, problem-solving, and basic skills, and their overall academic performance. They often show remarkable talents in areas that require reasoning and problem solving, yet they struggle with rote skills such as memorization of multiplication tables, spelling, and decoding. Although they may obtain excellent grades on classroom assignments, they perform poorly in more formal test situations. Because the majority of these students are now integrated into general education classrooms, every teacher must deal with the challenge of addressing the needs of children who learn differently. Furthermore, because each student has a unique learning style, teachers are required to address a broad range of learning needs within the classroom.

Strategies for Success provides realistic and accessible teaching techniques for teachers, special educators, and other professionals working with students at the late elementary, middle, and early high school levels. These strategies can help teachers to understand the diverse learning profiles of their students and create classroom environments that encourage all students to succeed. Classrooms that encourage effort, persistence, strategy use, goal orientation, and risk taking can often break the negative cycle of failure experienced by students such as Chris and Brandon, thus reducing their feelings of vulnerability and helplessness. Minor modifications in the classroom culture can often provide opportunities for students to realize their academic and social potential, as well as alleviate a great deal of misery and unnecessary frustration. Effective strategy use can enhance motivation, persistence, and self-concept and can consequently promote academic success and independent learning.

In these first two key chapters of this book, we provide an overview of the principles underlying strategy instruction. Chapter 1 addresses the following questions:

- Why should learning strategies be taught?
- What are the overall principles of classroom-based strategy instruction?
- How can strategies be taught most effectively?
- Do students need ongoing strategy instruction?
- How can teachers promote self-awareness and metacognition in the classroom?
- How can teachers recognize and understand different learning profiles?
- How can teachers recognize and understand students with learning and attentional difficulties?

Why Should Learning Strategies Be Taught?

Terms such as *learning strategies, teaching strategies,* and *strategic learning* are used widely to imply that learners can choose specific procedures for accomplishing particular tasks. These strategies can help students improve their reading, writing, math, and problem-solving performance. The importance of strategic learning has been demonstrated in work showing that successful learners use effective strategies to process information (Brown & Campione, 1986; Harris & Graham, 1992; Harris, Graham, & Mason, 2002; Meltzer, 1993b; Meltzer, Katzir, Miller, Reddy, & Roditi, 2004; Pressley, Goodchild, Fleet, Zajchowski, & Evans, 1989). Effective learning occurs when students' application of specific learning strategies interacts with a wide range of other processes, including automatic retrieval of basic skills, appropriate attention in the learning situation, self-awareness, motivation, and self-concept.

As shown in Figure 1.1, strategy instruction accomplishes the following goals:

- Students learn *how* to learn rather than only *what* to learn. In other words, students learn strategies that they can generalize across different content areas and different tasks.

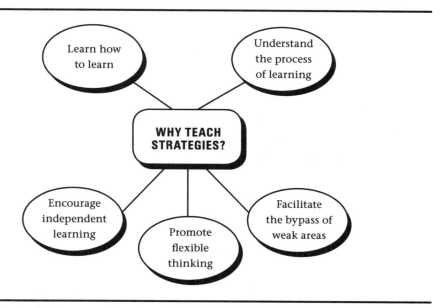

FIGURE 1.1. Goals of strategy instruction.

- Strategies help students begin to understand the process of learning.
- Strategies help students to bypass their areas of weakness and to perform at the level at which they are capable.
- Strategies promote flexible thinking and teach students the importance of shifting their approaches to different tasks.
- Strategies encourage independent learning.
- Strategy use helps students to become more efficient and more effective learners.

Learning strategies are particularly important for helping students to bypass their areas of weakness and to rely on their areas of competence. Students' willingness to apply strategies to their classwork and homework is therefore dependent on the extent to which they recognize the value of specific strategies. Students need to understand their own learning profiles and needs as learners and to recognize how and why strategies can help them attain academic success. Therefore, a critical ingredient for successful strategy instruction is each student's self-awareness of his or her profile of strengths and weaknesses, as well as the strategies that are most effective for his or her learning profile.

Students with learning difficulties are often inefficient as learners because they have difficulty prioritizing and identifying major themes. They frequently overfocus on details and show major organizational difficulties, which affect their rate and efficiency as learners. Although they may reach the same goals as their normally achieving peers, they often differ in how they get there, how fast they get there, and the frustration they experience en route. Just as a roundabout route to a destination can be frustrating because it

is very time consuming, so too can learning be frustrating when the process is long and arduous and the goal is not easily attainable.

How Can Strategies Be Taught Most Effectively?

Explicit strategy instruction is beneficial for all students, but it is essential for students with learning difficulties. Strategy instruction needs to be systematic, highly structured, and explicit, and should include opportunities for students to experience success as a result of using specific strategies. Strategy instruction is critical for teaching all students a broader range of strategies than they use spontaneously. Students need to be taught specific techniques for organizing and planning their work, and for memorizing, prioritizing, and self-checking (Institute for Learning and Development/ResearchILD and FableVision, 2001), which are all essential ingredients of academic success.

Several research-based strategy instruction methods have been shown to enhance learning for students with learning difficulties and can be easily incorporated into the general education classroom (Harris et al., 2002; Meltzer & Montague, 2001; Swanson, Hoskyn, & Lee, 1999). These methods include the following:

- Sequencing or breaking tasks into short activities and component tasks with step-by-step prompts that are gradually taken away

Overall Principles of Classroom-Based Strategy Instruction

- Every student learns differently and has a unique learning profile.
- Every student needs to understand his or her own profile of strengths and weaknesses.
- Every student must understand the importance of using strategies.
- Every student needs to understand the importance of hard work, persistence, and strategy use for academic success.
- Every student needs to understand that strategies require more effort at first but result in accurate and efficient work over time.
- Every student should develop personalized learning goals and a plan for using specific strategies to attain these goals.
- Every student needs opportunities to succeed as a result of using specific strategies and to recognize the link between the use of specific strategies and academic improvement.
- Every student needs opportunities to express his or her strengths and to develop an "island of competence" (Brooks, 1991) while using strategies.
- All students need to feel supported and connected in school so that their classrooms and schools engender a sense of belonging to a community where they are valued.

- Repetition, review, and practice in applying specific strategies
- Monitoring and adjusting the difficulty level and processing demands of the tasks
- Think-aloud modeling of successful task completion
- Creating small groups in the classroom for students to apply strategies and to discuss their successes and difficulties with their peers
- Involving special education teachers, tutors, and parents in strategy instruction
- Creating classroom climates in which all students value strategies and discuss novel strategies daily (e.g., creating a "Strategy-a-Day" board for students to add new strategies that they have used while doing homework)
- Providing students with frequent opportunities to practice the strategies they have learned and to apply these strategies to novel tasks
- Providing multistep grading systems so that students are graded for completion of different phases of their work and not only the final product (e.g., by breaking down a grade into component grades of the student's notes, outlines, drafts of written work, and the final product)

Do Students Need Ongoing Strategy Instruction?

Every grade level heralds changes in the curriculum, the setting, the expectations, and each student's cognitive and social development. Students' learning profiles are not static, but often change as a function of the match or mismatch between the student's specific strengths and weaknesses and the demands of the classroom, the teacher, and the curriculum. Some students who exhibit no early school difficulties may suddenly flounder when the classroom demands change and require the coordination of many different subskills and strategies. As a result, previously unrecognized learning difficulties may become evident in the later grades, when previously successful compensatory strategies are no longer effective.

Critical transition times in the curriculum—first grade, fourth grade, middle school, high school, and college—can be particularly problematic for students. Each of these transitions corresponds to increased organizational demands and the introduction of tasks that require the coordination and integration of multiple skills and strategies (e.g., complex writing assignments, book reports, and multiple-choice tests). Classroom teachers can help students to cope more successfully by teaching effective strategies and, where necessary, modifying the classroom demands to accommodate students' varying rates and styles of learning.

How Can Teachers Promote Self-Awareness and Metacognition in the Classroom?

Strategy instruction can be successful only when students are willing and able to generate strategies and to value and take ownership of the strategies they are taught. Students need to understand how they learn and how specific strategies can help them to improve their accuracy and eventual efficiency. Self-awareness is therefore essential for successful strategy instruction, which depends on students' understanding of their learning profiles and their willingness to make the effort needed to apply particular strategies to different learning tasks. Self-awareness is also important because of the increased work time involved initially as students learn new approaches. This process is often slow, and students need success before they generalize the strategies they have learned to a variety of tasks and types of work.

Although students achieve greater accuracy through the use of specific strategies, they may initially sacrifice speed and efficiency. Use of a systematic strategy, however, ensures that students become increasingly efficient over time, and this results in reduced work time (see Figure 1.2). For example, when students begin to use planning strategies to organize their written work, the time spent drawing maps and webs or developing three-column notes

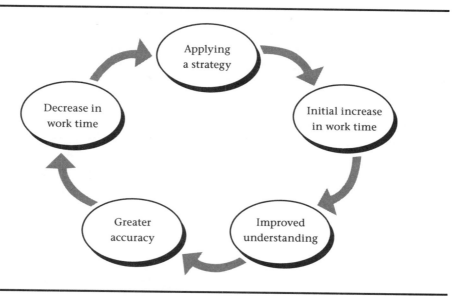

FIGURE 1.2. Applying a strategy.

may make students feel that they are spending more time on their written work; however, use of these strategies results in a written product that is more organized and requires less editing. As a result, written work eventually takes less time for students and results in better written products and higher grades. Therefore, a major challenge for teachers is to ensure that students who apply specific strategies achieve fairly rapid success. Classroom success increases students' willingness to use specific strategies and to make the effort to use the same strategies in different situations, the core component of generalization.

How Can Teachers Recognize and Understand Different Learning Profiles?

Teachers can use informal assessment methods to gain an understanding of why and how a particular student may be struggling. The idea of teachers as assessors is becoming increasingly popular as Assessment for Teaching methods are developed (Meltzer, 1993a, 1993b; Roditi, 1993). Both observations and a variety of classroom-based assessment methods can be used to evaluate how students learn the required material and how effectively they retain and access knowledge. Performance-based assessment techniques and portfolio assessment methods (Fuchs & Fuchs, 2002) have also become increasingly widespread for classroom assessment. A combination of these informal assessment methods can provide the skilled teacher with useful information about the strengths and weaknesses of most students.

Some students exhibit learning profiles that are difficult to understand without assessment information elicited from formal tests or classroom-based assessment measures. Formal neuropsychological and educational testing often provides essential information about a student's learning style and helps teachers to understand why a particular student is struggling in the classroom. However, these assessments cannot provide all the answers. It is important to recognize that assessments are limited when they provide only scores and grade-level equivalents. Furthermore, product-oriented tests do not clarify *how* the student is learning and *why* the student is experiencing difficulty. Assessments are most helpful when they are process oriented, focus on how the student learns, and provide specific educational recommendations that can be implemented in the classroom setting.

How Can Teachers Recognize and Understand Students with Learning and Attention Difficulties?

No single academic profile characterizes all students with learning difficulties who may have weaknesses in memory, language, auditory perception, visual perception, processing speed, or executive processes. Some are poor readers and spellers. Others have difficulty with written or oral expression. Still others cannot memorize math facts. Some students with learning difficulties may have weak organizational skills and may be erratic in their completion of homework assignments. Students with attention weaknesses may have both academic and social difficulties. The characteristic that all these students have in common is that, despite their average to above-average intellectual ability, they experience delays in reading, writing, mathematics, listening, and/or speaking skills. In other words, a significant discrepancy exists between ability and achievement. Most of these students have a combination of learning difficulties, the manifestation of which can vary enormously. Table 1.1 outlines the ways in which some students' learning difficulties may be exhibited in the classroom.

Many students with learning difficulties also experience attention difficulties and may show excessive impulsivity, distractibility, and motor activity. These students may experience organizational difficulties, have problems staying on task, and have difficulties concentrating in group situations. These behavioral characteristics often lead to a diagnosis of attention-deficit/hyperactivity disorder (ADHD).

Most elusive and confusing to teachers are the students who show attention problems but are not overactive. These students are often distractible, disorganized, or impulsive, and show poor self-monitoring skills. At times, they focus only on the global themes and ignore the details. At other times,

TABLE 1.1

How Learning Difficulties Manifest in the Classroom

Learning Difficulties That Students Experience	How Students Demonstrate These Difficulties in the Classroom
• May process information in unique ways • May process information at very slow rates • May have language-processing weaknesses • May have difficulties remembering rote information due to weaknesses in automatic memory • May not develop efficient and effective strategies for completing work	• Demonstrate discrepancies between in-class and test performance • Are slow to volunteer, have difficulty with timed tasks • Have difficulty following directions, appear inattentive • Struggle to remember letter formations, math facts, days of the week, months of the year • Seem to lag behind others and are slower at mastering strategies for learning; difficulties often mask the students' superior conceptual reasoning and problem solving
• May have difficulty shifting flexibly among different approaches • May not abandon strategies that are inefficient or ineffective • May struggle to prioritize and to focus on salient details	• Have difficulty adjusting to new teachers and new situations • May consistently solve problems the same way despite instruction in alternate strategies • May talk around issues; cannot summarize; have poor study skills, poor outlining strategies, poor reading comprehension
• May be disorganized or may use different processing routes to organize information • May have difficulty coordinating the strategies needed to learn effectively	• Have messy book bags, have disorganized writing, are unprepared for classes • Demonstrate inconsistent task performance (e.g., score 100% on structured spelling tests with single dictated words, but misspell these same words in the context of creative writing)
• Unaware of the usefulness of specific planning and checking strategies • May be impulsive and may not spontaneously plan their work • May not spontaneously self-correct	• Do not use prereading or prewriting strategies, do not edit • Are disorganized, have difficulty budgeting their time • Are careless with math, spelling, and writing

Note. Specific classroom management strategies for students with LD are listed throughout this book. This list includes only selected difficulties that students experience.

they overfocus on details and have difficulty identifying global issues. They consequently become confused when too much information is presented. They are also extremely distractible and may appear to daydream so that instructions often need to be repeated. As a result, tasks that require organization and prioritizing may be difficult for them. Because they do not have behavior problems and their difficulties are often subtle, they may be ignored or misdiagnosed. As a result, their academic problems may be incorrectly attributed to low motivation, lack of effort, or lowered intellectual ability rather than to their attention problems. Table 1.2 provides strategies for assisting students with ADHD in the classroom.

For students with learning and attention difficulties, strategy instruction needs to be explicit, structured, and recursive. Frequent use of strategies across content areas and in a variety of settings (e.g., home, school) allows for consolidation and generalization. Strategy use and practice should be required for in-class and homework assignments. Small-group instruction within the larger classroom can often provide opportunities for practice and mastery of strategies, whereas large-group classroom-based instruction ensures that generalization occurs. The goal is to ensure that students learn to use strategies flexibly in different domains and with different tasks.

TABLE 1.2

Strategies To Assist Students wth Attention Problems in the Classroom

Difficulties Students with Attention Problems Experience	How Students Demonstrate These Difficulties in Classroom	Strategies To Assist Students with Attention Problems
Distractibility	Daydream (distracted by inner thoughts) or attend to extraneous sounds or visual stimuli in the class-room	Make eye contact with students; check in with students frequently
Impulsivity	Do not plan before begin-ning tasks Have social problems because of inappropriate comments Appear careless and inattentive to details	Provide preferential seating Teach planning and self-checking strategies (e.g., personalized checklists)
Disorganization	Lose work, forget homework, do not complete assignments	Teach organizational strategies (e.g., calendars, homework notebooks) Check homework regu-larly, ask parents to check homework
Difficulty sustaining attention	Have difficulty following through on long-term assignments Have difficulty concentrating during classes with lecture formats May struggle to focus	Break down long-term projects into manageable steps Provide hands-on projects Use cooperative learning Accompany oral presenta-tions with visuals
Fidgetiness and motoric activity	Are fidgety, move around, fiddle with objects	Provide students with legitimate opportunities to move around (e.g., chalkboard monitor, messenger)
Inconsistent performance	Have inconsistent work quality across tasks, settings, and situations Repeat the same mistakes	Accept the variability in students' performance

Note. (a) Many, but not all, students with attentional problems are diagnosed with attention-deficit dis-order. (b) This list includes only a few selected strategies; later chapters provide more detailed suggestions.

Chapter 2

Techniques for Teaching Learning Strategies

Einstein used the most sophisticated math to develop his theories, but often his sums would not come out right. He had trouble learning facts, words, and texts, but he was teacher to the world. He was slow to speak, but, in time, the world listened.

—West, 1997, p. 129

Like Albert Einstein, most students do not spontaneously access their learning strengths to bypass their areas of weakness and to maximize their effort and organization in response to the numerous demands of the classroom. This difficulty becomes increasingly problematic as students advance through the grades. When students reach middle school, they are required to meet the demands of many teachers who may have varying styles of instruction and different performance standards. Thus, the strategies they learn are critically important in helping students to become more effective, efficient, and independent as learners, as well as more organized in school and at home.

As a teacher, you are the single most valuable resource available to your students. Therefore, you will want to maximize the time you spend with your students, whether in small- or large-group instructional settings or in one-to-one situations. Strategy instruction allows you to optimize your instructional time in the classroom by helping students to gain insights into the learning process and fostering greater independence.

● ●

The Three Keys to Student Success: Positive Self-Concept, Effective Strategy Use, and Focused Effort

The most important thing I learned was a combination of two things: One was learning the strategies. The other thing was learning that you have to learn how to learn.

—D., high school senior

Have you ever wondered about the impact of your feedback and expectations on your students' self-concepts and academic performance? Our research findings have shown a cyclical relationship between teachers' judgments, students' self-perceptions, and students' academic performance. Our studies to date have also demonstrated that hard work and an inordinate number of hours spent studying will not, *on their own,* result in academic success for students with a range of learning challenges. Rather, students need to learn to work hard and to use *effective strategies* that help them to bypass the impact of their learning challenges so that they can show what they know in the classroom and on tests. When these students use effective strategies during the many hours they spend studying, their use of strategies results in academic success, which in turn enhances motivation and effort. This results in more efficient and successful academic performance irrespective of the existence of learning difficulties (Meltzer, 1996; Meltzer, Katzir-Cohen, Miller, & Roditi, 2001; Meltzer, Reddy, Pollica, Roditi, et al., 2004). Effort, strategy use, and a positive self-concept are therefore critical interconnected processes that help all students to attain the academic success that they are capable of and they deserve (see Figure 2.1).

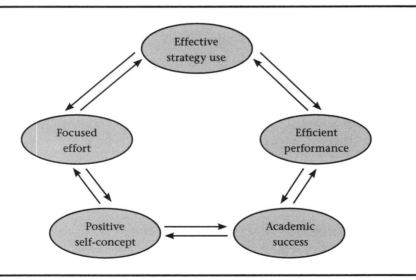

FIGURE 2.1. Strategy–effort cycle.

Strategy use and effort in five cognitive domains are critical for learning: organization, memory, prioritizing, cognitive flexibility, and self-monitoring or checking. Ideally, instruction should focus on teaching strategies in these five different cognitive domains. These strategies help students to learn how to learn and to recognize the important phases in the learning process as steps toward the final goal or end point. Strategies also help students to become lifelong learners as a result of understanding their individual learning profiles and reflecting on their approaches to a variety of different learning tasks.

What Principles Guide Strategy Instruction?

Strategy instruction can be readily incorporated into the classroom when the curriculum content is used as a springboard for teaching students how to learn. When you begin to teach strategies in your classroom, you will find that the processes that students use to remember, think, problem solve, organize, plan, self-check, and self-monitor become as important as the content they need to learn. Effective learning strategies help all students learn *how* to learn and, furthermore, can be taught within the context of the daily curriculum. Figure 2.2 depicts the interconnectedness of these learning strategies.

Students with learning and attention problems need strategy instruction that is explicit and provides consistent practice, repetition, and review. Some of the principles underlying strategy instruction are listed in Table 2.1.

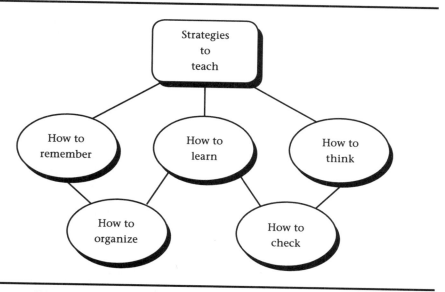

FIGURE 2.2. Strategies for teaching.

TABLE 2.1

Principles Underlying Strategy Instruction

- Encourage active learning (e.g., prereading, prewriting, cooperative learning groups).

- Review concepts and principles.

- Use a spiraled method of instruction (preface new material with review of previous work).

- Teach strategies in the context of the curriculum and not as a separate topic. For example, when students are required to complete independent research for a science project, teach strategies for highlighting, note taking, and organizing information.

- Teach strategies through modeling and direct explanations of procedures.

- Provide as much practice and review as possible so that students can apply the strategies they learn to a variety of different examples (e.g., strategies for active reading are practiced with science, social studies, history).

- Monitor students' practice in applying different strategies and provide helpful feedback.

- Teach preplanning and organizational strategies.

- Teach self-monitoring and self-checking strategies.

- Help students to experience mastery and success so that they understand the benefits of using specific strategies. This will ensure that they value the strategy, use it consistently, and generalize the strategy to other tasks and settings.

- Communicate and collaborate with all involved professionals.

- Encourage continued use of and generalization of strategies.

- Emphasize the importance of automaticity in basic skills (math facts, spelling).

Note. Students with unique learning needs often need more repetition, greater intensity, and more structure when strategy instruction occurs.

© 2006 by PRO-ED, Inc.

Classroom-based strategy instruction can be implemented using the following simple suggestions.

 Think big, start small. Once you have adopted a "strategic" approach to accommodating the many different learning styles in your classroom, you will use this philosophy to make decisions about the way your class is structured. Keep in mind that change occurs gradually, over time. Introduce a few new strategies that you feel are most critical to the needs of your students. Make a few modifications for those students who need them the most. When you feel comfortable with these, attempt a new strategy and add a few more modifications.

Over time, you will develop a repertoire of strategies and modifications to use with the entire class or with individual students. Your goal is to encourage your students to create their own strategies eventually, and to share these with each other.

→ ***Individualizing does* not *mean making multiple lesson plans.*** The idea behind strategic teaching is to make efficient use of *your* time as well as your students' effort. Because strategies are best taught in context, strategy instruction is integrated into your existing curriculum. This may require some modifications, rather than additions, to your present plans and materials. In other words, you can be strategic in the approach you take to all that you do, including classroom seating and standardized testing.

→ ***"Do what I say* and *do what I do."*** One of the most effective and efficient ways to make your classroom a setting for strategic learning is to model strategic thinking processes for your students. Thinking aloud as you solve a problem offers your students a unique opportunity to witness problem-solving strategies in action. Too often, students think teachers have all the answers, but they have no idea how teachers arrive at those answers. Your example can heighten students' awareness of their own metacognitive processes.

→ ***Question your questions.*** Think about your questioning techniques in the classroom. In addition to assessing students' knowledge of the content material, you can also engage your students in questions that will lead them to understand the processes involved in acquiring new information. For example, when a student gives a correct answer to a content question, you can probe further by asking, "How did you arrive at that answer?" Your students will be encouraged to find that there are numerous ways to locate information. Alerting students to the processes involved in knowledge acquisition can lead them to be more efficient learners.

What Is the Role of Organization in the Learning Process?

As students advance into the fourth grade and beyond, an increasing emphasis is placed on long-term projects, independent work, book reports, and tasks that require planning, prioritizing, and organization. Many students begin to experience school problems for the first time and may show a range of organizational difficulties that often have a significant impact on their academic performance. These organizational difficulties affect students' ability to plan, prioritize, and coordinate the many diverse requirements of the curriculum from the upper elementary grades onward.

Organizational Difficulties That Affect Classroom Performance

- Students may have difficulty organizing and budgeting their time.
- Students may have trouble planning independently.
- Students may struggle to coordinate short-term and long-term assignments.
- Students may need help to ensure that they continue to use organizational procedures in a sustained and systematic manner.
- Students may not record their homework assignments consistently.
- Students may write down their homework assignments but forget their notebooks.
- Students may write down their homework assignments but forget the necessary books and papers at school.
- Students may complete their homework assignments but forget to hand them in to their teachers.
- Students' desks, lockers, and book bags may be so messy and disorganized that they have trouble finding their belongings.
- Work may be late or incomplete because of students' slow rate of processing.
- Students' work may seem messy; papers often may be crumpled or may show frequent erasures and cross-outs.
- The work students submit may not reflect their level of effort.

How Can You Improve the Organizational Strategies of Your Students?

By incorporating a few simple techniques in the daily curriculum, teachers can help students to develop more efficient work habits and to improve their organizational skills. These organizational strategies are important for all students and are particularly critical for students with learning and attention difficulties. Before they use these strategies independently, students with learning and attention problems often need more structure, repetition, review, and reminders than do other students.

Organizational Strategies

- *Planning Calendars.* Teach students to record major project deadlines, goals and plans for completing different phases of each project, and associated due dates. Allocate time for students to write their assignments in their planners.

(continues)

Organizational Strategies
Continued.

▥ *Homework Notebooks.* Teach students to record their homework assignments and a list of the books they need to take home. They should also check off the assignments after they complete their work and place them in their school bags.

▥ *Planning Long-term Projects.* Teach students to budget their work time by providing phased timelines and study plans. For example, they could estimate and record the amount of time needed for a particular assignment. After completing the assignment, they could compare the actual and budgeted time and then use this discrepancy to guide future time allocations.

▥ *Organization.* Teach students systems for organizing their desks and lockers at school.

▥ *Test Preparation.* Teach short- and long-term planning strategies.

▥ *Notebooks and Folders.* Remember that different systems work for different students. For example, some students are successful with folders that are color-coded by subject, whereas others are systematic enough to use trapper keepers.

▥ *Color Coding.* Teach students to color-code materials for each class. The same color can be used for textbook covers, folders, and notebook covers in each subject (e.g., red for social studies, green for math).

▥ *Checklists.* Teach students to tape checklists of items needed for each class to the front panel of the binder or folder used in that class.

▥ *Homework Hotline.* Create a hotline that is based on either voice mail or a Web page. This allows students to double-check their homework assignments if they cannot record the assignments rapidly enough in their planners or if they are absent from class. Web sites such as http://www.schoolnotes.com allow teachers to create their own Web sites for listing homework assignments and upcoming events.

▥ *Homework on the Web.* Create a schoolwide Web site that includes homework assignments routinely updated by teachers.

The following organizational strategies may also be helpful:

• Encourage students to try different organizers and organizational systems. Remember that individualized modifications may be needed for many students.

- Enforce the use of homework notebooks, which should be signed by parents and teachers daily. Students with learning difficulties require accountability and regular routines. These students often need reminders long after other students use these methods spontaneously. Remember that checking a student's homework notebook does not discourage independence but simply helps students to develop a routine and a systematic approach to homework.
- Give your students a homework jumpstart and allocate the last 5 to 8 minutes of every lesson for homework review. This will help students to clarify their questions and confusion and to approach their work in a more organized fashion.
- Help your students to list their plans and priorities for multi-step assignments. Modeling will help them schedule their work more easily and improve their time management.
- Teach students to develop their own personalized checklists for checking, correcting, and editing their work. Encourage them to paste these checklists into their notebooks.
- Teach your students strategies for note taking (two-column notes, three-column notes with strategies listed, mapping, and webbing) and review these note-taking methods frequently.
- Remember that students with language-processing weaknesses often benefit from visual strategies such as maps and webs that summarize all critical information on a single page. However, students with weaknesses in visual processing become confused when complex graphic organizers are used, and they benefit from systems that are more language oriented (e.g., two-column notes). For these reasons, it is important to expose your students to a variety of methods and to allow each student to select a system that addresses his or her specific learning styles (see later chapters in this book for more details).
- Teach your students outlining techniques because these reinforce structure, highlight major themes, and provide categories for organizing information. Remember that students with learning and attention problems may need more extensive review and practice with these techniques.

Strategic Classroom Organization

Teachers can help students with learning problems through classroom organization. The following strategies are useful for this purpose.

➡ *Implement preferential seating when necessary.* Be aware of each student's level of involvement during different tasks. Are your students all actively engaged in the lesson, or is the dialogue primarily confined to a core set of students? During independent work periods, are students completing the assignment accurately and efficiently? Some students may benefit from preferential seating to accommodate their learning styles. For example, students with language-processing difficulties may need to be closer to the teacher, where they can pick up visual cues and receive redirection when necessary. Students with attention weaknesses may need to be seated away from noisy or distracting areas of the classroom. In fact, you may want to group students' desks according to their learning profiles. Remember to establish eye contact with students, especially when you circulate around the room.

➡ *Use flexible groupings for strategy instruction.* Placing students in smaller groups for instruction is a common instructional practice. Often, the criteria for these groups has been ability level (e.g., low, middle, high). With flexible groupings, students can be grouped and disbanded for various purposes. Students can be grouped in one way to learn a specific skill or strategy. Another set of groups can be formed according to the strategies students prefer to use for a given task. Alternatively, you might teach two strategies for the same task and then divide the class into groups, with each group trying one strategy. Students could then report on the benefits and drawbacks of that strategy to the larger group. As different students report their reasons for preferring one strategy over another, they are also giving you information about their learning styles.

➡ *Use strategy practice labs.* Practice labs provide students the opportunity to apply the different strategies you have taught them. With practice, many strategies can become automatic, and students will also begin to see the efficacy of certain strategies for specific tasks. Designate one class period per week as strategy lab time and allow the students to experiment with a learning strategy that is useful for your content material.

➡ *Capitalize on seatwork opportunities.* It is important that students learn to apply strategies independently and with confidence. Purposeful, well-directed seatwork can be a vehicle for strategy instruction. In addition to allowing you to check students' recall of information, seatwork can also include instruction in the use of strategies. Seatwork allows you time to work with individual students, while providing the students with practice in critical thinking skills for independent work.

➡ *Use checklists and contracts.* Checklists help students assume additional responsibility for their academic progress and behavior. Create checklists with your students that target a few key goals. State expectations in positive terms (e.g., "Will turn in rough draft of assignment on Friday" instead of "Will not turn in assignments late," or "Will check capitalization on each paper" instead of "Will not make punctuation errors"). Design the checklists for success by setting reasonable goals that you and your students agree are attainable. Alter or add to the checklists as the students master the initial goals. Permit your students to earn rewards, such as free time or computer time, for their progress.

Contracts are similar to checklists and offer another way to assist your students in becoming more self-directed. Once you and a student have decided on the terms for a contract, student and teacher responsibilities are outlined in writing. Both sign the agreement, which is designed to be reviewed at certain times. As with the checklists, rewards are specified. Both systems allow students to develop responsibility and control over their academic progress and behavior.

→ *Make classroom assignments strategic.* Simple modifications to assignments can dramatically enhance the strategic instruction in your classroom. Examples of modifications are as follows:

- Modify worksheet instructions to emphasize strategic thinking. In this way, you can keep the same materials but alter the focus of the lesson from straight recall to process thinking (i.e., from testing to teaching).
- Consider assigning fewer math problems or English exercises and redirecting the additional time to the practice of strategies in that specific content area.
- Provide a systematic and consistent structure for giving and recording classroom assignments. Use multiple methods to assign homework. Explain the assignment. Write the assignment on the board and give students time to write it down in their notebooks. Insist that students write it down. If possible, insist they maintain some form of an assignment notebook. Implement random homework checks and grade homework assignments in these instances. If possible, list assignments on your school's Web site or develop a homework hotline.
- Assign different levels of homework (e.g., Level 1 is independent work, Level 2 is working with a classmate, and Level 3 is getting help from a parent or tutor).
- Give students opportunities to hand in their test corrections as a homework assignment. This allows them to learn from their mistakes and raise their test grades.

→ *Make accommodations for individual learning needs.* Students who have difficulty with their rate of work or the motor demands of writing may need to use the word processor and be given extended time for certain writing requirements or lengthy written projects. Involve the students in the process of determining these modifications and clearly articulate your expectations. Make it clear that different learning styles warrant different levels of accommodations and that the eventual goals and expectations are the same for all students even though the process involved in attaining these goals may differ.

Students with reading difficulties may need other modifications. For example, students with good conceptualization abilities but significant decoding weaknesses may benefit from listening to their textbooks on tape (available from Recordings for the Blind and Dyslexic [http://www.rfbd.org]). (See Appendix C for additional suggestions.)

➡ ***Collaborate with team members.*** Communication among teachers is a major key to success for many students with learning difficulties. Find out what your colleagues are expecting from the students. Whenever possible, coordinate your demands with those of other teachers. Try not to schedule major due dates within the same week. Find out how your students are doing in other classes. You may find that a student who struggles in your class is successful in another class. Incorporate into your teaching those elements of another teacher's style or strategies that are effective with a particular student. Also, share insights about successes you have had with a student that can assist another teacher who is struggling with the same student. Organize regular meetings to ensure that all teachers use a team approach for addressing the needs of students with learning problems.

➡ ***Take a proactive approach when communicating with parents.*** Parents often struggle at home when helping their children complete homework and study for tests. Offer guidelines to parents at the beginning of the school year about your expectations regarding their involvement.

- Tell parents how much help they should give and how much time homework should be expected to take.
- Offer suggestions as to how parents can set up an optimal homework environment at home (e.g., a study space free of distractions, a routine for homework completion).
- Teach students study strategies and inform parents about the ways in which they can help students to apply these strategies at home (e.g., with a question-and-answer format, parents can ask their children the questions). Encourage parents to contact you via e-mail if students are having problems with homework demands, and make modifications as appropriate.
- Whenever possible, inform parents when students have improved in their strategy use. Too often, parents hear from

teachers only when difficulties arise. Informing parents of positive achievements will encourage them to remain involved and enhance the student's self-esteem.

- Whenever possible, inform parents in the early stages about problems that appear in learning and behavior. When a problem develops, it is always best to "nip it in the bud" before it becomes too difficult to remediate. Contacting the parent may provide insight into the nature of the problem and assist you in developing effective solutions. This also indicates to the student that all adults are working together as a team.

- For some students, communication with parents is very helpful and can prevent the development of problem situations. E-mail, calls, conferences, or communication notebooks often provide efficient communication systems between teachers and parents. Teachers, parents, and older students can agree about the frequency of communication (e.g., every day, once a week) and record pertinent information, accentuating any positive improvements.

➔   ***Focus on the process as well as the end product.*** Allow students to complete projects in a process-oriented fashion. In other words, break long-term assignments into smaller units and set goals and deadlines for each phase. Develop study plans with students to help them accomplish each goal. Collect and assess students' work throughout the project, rather than solely at completion. This process will allow you to gauge students' understanding of the assignment and their progress toward completion. You will also learn quickly which students need additional direction or lack specific skills needed to complete sections of an assignment. This strategy can save you precious time in grading the final outcome, as well as alleviate the frustration of many students with learning difficulties who may work diligently but without the strategies they need. At other times, you may want to allow students to have the option of submitting selected drafts of their work prior to the completed assignments.

➔   ***Allow some freedom of choice.*** Remember that no one strategy works for everyone. Make available a variety of organizational templates (e.g., different types of maps, webs, two-column note-taking systems). Allowing students to choose a strategy engages them in the learning process and encourages them to consider their thinking and learning in a new and hopefully more purposeful manner.

➔   ***Be direct. Be strategic. Keep it simple.*** Keep in mind the importance of being direct with students about the *how* of learning, in addition to the *what* of learning. If you and your students are to be successful with strategy instruction, it is also important to keep the task simple. Teach only a few strategies at a time and allow many opportunities for the practice and generalization of each strategy.

• •

Empowering Students To Become Independent Learners and Self-Advocates

Self-awareness is a critical component of successful strategy instruction, as students must be willing to make the effort necessary to apply a specific strategy consistently. The success of strategy instruction is also influenced by students' ability to value and own the strategies they are taught. This ensures that they will expend the effort necessary for learning new routines. Students' recognition of the value of using specific strategies is also extremely important due to the initial increase in work time that is involved as students learn new routines. For example, when students begin to use a planning strategy to organize their written output (e.g., drawing maps and webs), there is an initial increase in work time. Speed and efficiency are sacrificed to attain greater accuracy. However, use of a systematic method ensures that students become increasingly efficient over time, which eventually decreases their work time. One of the most difficult challenges of strategy instruction, therefore, is to help students to develop the self-awareness and self-knowledge to be patient and to delay gratification during the learning phase. Fairly rapid success as a result of using a strategy usually helps students to value specific strategies and to expend the necessary effort to use these strategies. This recognition of the value and utility of a strategy leads, in turn, to maintenance and generalization of the strategy.

To help students to become independent learners and self-advocates, it is, therefore, important that you understand their perceptions of their own abilities and their views of the strategies that they use to accomplish different academic tasks. Consider these questions:

- Do they have realistic judgments of the important components of classroom learning?
- Do they recognize the importance of using specific strategies?
- Do they use different strategies for completing various academic tasks?

Some students recognize the importance of using specific learning strategies, whereas other students do not implement any strategies as they complete different academic tasks. Clearly, these students will perceive strategy instruction through different lenses.

How Do Students Judge Their Own Abilities?

Students can become independent learners only when (a) they understand their learning profiles, (b) they maintain positive views of their own competence, and (c) they are aware of the unique demands of different learning situations. Self-awareness is a critical precursor to the strategies that underlie effective learning—namely, planning, monitoring, checking, and evaluating outcomes. Students' use of particular strategies also is associated with their feelings of empowerment in the learning situation and their willingness to invest the effort needed to use the strategies that are important for success.

Self-esteem and motivation also affect the learning process in very important ways and often interact with students' willingness to apply strategies to their schoolwork. Successful learners frequently attribute their successes to effort and their failures to lack of effort, and are therefore more likely to use strategies actively. In contrast, students with learning difficulties often experience consistent failure over the years, which negatively affects their self-perceptions and self-esteem. Some students believe they are "dumb" and attribute their failure to insufficient ability rather than limited effort or different learning styles (Licht, 1993). As a result of this "learned helplessness," they may become anxious and fearful of failure, with the result that they are unlikely to use active problem-solving strategies and may avoid challenging tasks (Licht, 1993).

Classroom-Based Assessment: A Critical Ingredient of Successful Strategy Instruction

Teachers and other professionals can evaluate students' perceptions of their approach to learning through classroom-based assessment. One useful tool is the *Strategy Observation System* (SOS; Meltzer, Katzir, Miller, Reddy, & Roditi, 2004; Meltzer, Houser, Perlman, & Roditi, 1998; Meltzer, Roditi, & Stein, 1998), a series of questionnaires designed by the staff at ResearchILD to identify students' and teachers' perceptions of strategic learning. The SOS includes two questionnaires: the Student Self-Report System (SSRS) and the Teacher Observation System (TOS). This set of questionnaires assesses teachers' judgments of students' strategy use, as well as students' self-perceptions of their own strategy use.

The SSRS samples students' views of their learning strategies and work habits in reading, writing, spelling, math, and general organization. The SSRS has been used in a large study as part of the Strategies for Success program (Meltzer, Katzir, et al., 2004; Meltzer, Roditi, & Stein, 1998). This system can help you understand your students' judgments of their ability and strategies.

Sample Items from the SSRS

- After I read, I try to tell the story in my own words.
- When I read, I ask myself questions to help me remember.
- Before I begin to read my textbook, I look at the headings and pictures to get an idea about what I will be reading.
- When I have to write a paper for school, I don't know where to begin.
- Before I write, I plan my ideas on paper.
- When I am writing, I forget how to spell words.
- I use tricks to help me remember math facts.
- I have a step-by-step plan before I start solving a math word problem.
- I check my work before turning it in.
- I make a plan before I begin my homework.

The TOS provides teachers with a method of rating students' strategy use systematically. The TOS helps teachers observe and analyze students' efficiency and flexibility in strategic learning, as well as their self-monitoring strategies. Teachers observe students' learning strategies and work habits in reading, writing, spelling, math, and general organization. The TOS is closely linked to the SSRS so that comparisons between teacher and student perceptions can be made.

Sample Items from the TOS

- Readily completes reading assignments.
- Uses outlines to organize writing.
- Completed work has been proofread for spelling and punctuation.
- Corrects spelling errors systematically.
- Uses strategies (e.g., pictures) to solve word problems.
- Comes to class prepared.

Both the SSRS and the TOS have been used in a number of Massachusetts school systems, and the findings of a number of studies have been reported previously (Meltzer et al., 2001). Teacher comments have indicated that these surveys provide information that is extremely helpful for understanding the strategies used by students in the learning situation. Inventories such as these can help teachers understand and address the diverse needs of students in their classrooms.

How Can You Help All Students To Become Effective Strategic Learners?

- Help all students to understand their profiles of strengths and weaknesses in the learning situation. Students with learning difficulties need to recognize that their strong intellectual ability will help them to overcome their processing weaknesses and that their academic struggles bear no relationship to their intelligence.
- Ensure that all students experience success in at least one area; this will help them believe in the value of hard work and recognize that their efforts will lead to success.
- Encourage students to understand the importance of taking risks in different learning situations.
- Help students to understand the importance of shifting strategies and approaches based on the situational and task demands.
- Help students to recognize the essential role of self-correcting and self-checking and help them learn to implement appropriate strategies.
- Help students develop personalized checklists to correct their work.
- Encourage students to request preferential seating if they experience difficulty concentrating or processing the oral directions in a group setting.
- Encourage students to move to a quiet part of the classroom if necessary.
- Encourage students to discuss their homework assignments at appropriate times with you or their classmates.
- Help students to believe in themselves and to recognize themselves as active, independent learners.
- Encourage students to discuss their learning difficulties and to self-advocate with all teachers so that appropriate accommodations can be implemented (e.g., extended time on tests, multiple forms of evaluation opportunities for extra-credit work).

Strategy Instruction in the Context of Standards-Based Testing

Test results are the gateway to school success, graduation, college entry, and job advancement. Poor test performance can bar students from many important opportunities that would otherwise enable them to realize their potential. As state-mandated testing is now a requirement for school graduation in most states, students are at greater risk for failing in school if they lack effective test-taking strategies. When test performance can mean the difference between a

B and a D, or between advancing to high school or repeating a grade, the critical need for test-taking strategies for all students is self-evident.

Instruction in test-taking strategies is important in view of the demanding curriculum standards and the pressure on all students to learn how to express their ideas coherently and persuasively and to perform optimally in test situations. Many students, especially those with learning and attention problems, lack "test-wiseness," or facility with test-taking strategies, and their grades on tests do not reflect their understanding of the content, the extent of their preparation, or their level of ability. These students need systematic instruction in strategies that help them to remember the information they learn, to organize their ideas systematically, to apply a variety of different approaches to different tasks, and to check their work.

In the classroom, all students benefit from learning strategies in five critical cognitive processes:

- Memorizing
- Organizing
- Prioritizing
- Shifting approaches
- Checking and self-monitoring

Strategies in each of these cognitive areas help students to improve their efficiency and accuracy during the three stages of studying and test taking. Students need to learn strategies that help them to master these three stages and to apply appropriate strategies *before, during,* and *after* a test (see Figure 2.3). These systematic, multimodal strategies help students to become metacognitive learners who understand how they learn best and who are willing to work hard to become strategic learners.

An easy-to-use, systematic approach to teaching students strategies in these five areas is incorporated in BrainCogs. BrainCogs, an interactive, media-rich CD-ROM program developed by the Institute for Learning and Development/ResearchILD and FableVision, is designed to help students to develop strategies for learning, studying, and successful test taking and to apply strategies that best match their learning profiles (http://www.fablevision .com/braincogs).

In the classroom, you can use BrainCogs to help your students to learn how to organize, prioritize, integrate, and retrieve information while they simultaneously learn the required content. They also learn when to use which strategies in which contexts. You can use the software to teach students how to organize their materials when they study and complete homework, how to prioritize and figure out what is most important to study, how to shift flexibly among different strategies, how to analyze questions on tests and in work assignments, and how to check their answers in their written work. These 13 strategies are taught in the context of real-life situations and are applicable to a broad range of tasks and content areas. For more information about Brain-Cogs, see Appendix A.1.

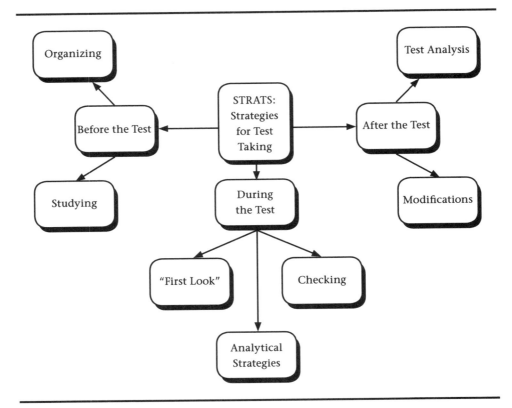

FIGURE 2.3. Strategies for test taking.

· ·

Conclusion

Explicit strategy instruction can play a critical role in helping *all* students to learn and perform more successfully. When a holistic approach to learning is integrated within the context of classroom work, students with a diverse range of learning needs are empowered to show what they know in all learning situations. Classroom-based strategy instruction teaches students to value the learning process. It unravels the mystery of how students learn new information, recall previously learned information, and approach assignments and tests. Students are encouraged to discover their learning styles and to employ learned information to their advantage in the classroom and at home. Independence is supported as students become increasingly more aware of the benefits of strategy use and feel motivated to continue to use techniques that work for them. Perhaps most important, students begin to view themselves as capable learners who can weather the daily challenges and demands of the school curriculum.

Chapter 3

Reading, Decoding, Fluency, and Spelling

I ... learned the importance of strategies, and that it wasn't about being stupid.... There were different ways to learn.... I was in the best reading group after I learned that.

—David, 16 years old

Why Teach Strategies in Decoding and Spelling?

We know from recent research that skillful readers possess a subset of skills and abilities that include phonological awareness, sound–symbol correspondence, decoding, word recognition, fluency, automatic retrieval, and language comprehension (Adams, 1990). We also know that students with reading disabilities, who have a great deal of difficulty acquiring one or more of these skills, struggle to learn early reading and spelling skills. Early identification and intervention are therefore necessary to reduce the incidence and severity of reading disabilities.

Phonological Awareness and Reading

Recent research on reading indicates that *phonological awareness*—that is, the awareness of distinct sounds within words and the ability to manipulate these sounds—is associated with early reading success. In fact, phonological aware-ness may be one of the best predictors of early reading success (Stanovich, 1986). Children learn phonological awareness through activities such as rhyming, segmenting words or word groups into smaller parts, and generating words from a given sound.

To become independent readers, students must learn to decode un-familiar words. This can be accomplished through direct instruction of the phonological rules or indirectly through deduction. Many, although not all, students with strong phonological awareness appear to acquire early reading skills easily. These students are able to play with sounds and syllables, and to infer and remember sound–symbol relationships, regardless of the read-ing methods used. Typically, these same students show strengths in spelling because they can rely on their knowledge or memory of sound–symbol cor-respondence rules to write words. Students with learning difficulties typically do not readily make these inferences. They may have difficulty segmenting words into sounds or syllables, remembering syllable types and rules, and gen-eralizing the variations in phoneme production. These difficulties often result in reading and spelling problems. Weaknesses in visual memory and auto-matic memory also have an impact on reading and spelling development.

Early intervention and prevention are important for reducing the number of students with reading and spelling difficulties. Even if the difficul-ties are identified at a later age, however, use of systematic, multisensory, pho-netic remediation and intervention can still be effective. Older students may require more intensive remediation in conjunction with strategy instruction that helps them to bypass their difficulties.

Naming Speed and Reading

In addition to phonological processing deficits, many children who struggle to read also exhibit difficulties with naming speed. Naming speed difficulties appear to reflect problems with automaticity and rapid retrieval of informa-tion such as letter patterns. These problems can affect students' word identi-fication skills and compromise their reading fluency and comprehension. These students need explicit instruction in rapid orthographic (letter pattern) recognition and retrieval, vocabulary development, and phonological analysis and blending skills.

Determining Whether Decoding Is a Problem

Weaknesses in decoding are often difficult to detect in the fourth grade and beyond because most in-class reading occurs silently. Weaknesses in decoding can and should be remediated, and the earlier these difficulties are detected, the better. Therefore, it is important to determine whether a student is having difficulty with decoding at the beginning of each school year. Take each student aside *individually* and ask him or her to read aloud from a grade-level text. It is essential that this informal assessment be done on an individual basis to ensure that no student is embarrassed in front of his or her peers. If the student has difficulty reading aloud or rereads words, lines, and paragraphs in order to comprehend, it is important to gather information to uncover the root of the difficulty. There are many reasons why a student may have difficulty with decoding. To determine what type of instruction or remediation the student will best respond to, you must first discover the cause of the decoding problem. Assess each of the following areas.

➡ *Phonological Awareness.* Consider the following critical questions.
1. Can the student rhyme?
   - Orally present rhyming and nonrhyming words and ask the student whether the words rhyme.
   - Orally present one word and ask the student to produce a rhyming word.
2. Can the student create new words by eliminating the following sounds?
   - a syllable in a compound word ("Say *cobweb;* now say it without the *cob*")
   - a syllable at the beginning or end of a word ("Say *depart;* now say it without the *de*" or "Say *invite;* now say it without the *vite*")
   - a beginning sound ("Say *stop;* now say it without the /s/")
   - an ending sound ("Say *stain;* now say it without the /n/")
   - a part of a blend ("Say *glow;* now say it without the /l/")

➡ *Knowledge of Sound–Symbol Correspondence.* Write each phoneme (consonant, short and long vowel, digraph, diphthong) on a separate index card, and ask the student to tell you what sound the letter(s) make.

➡ *Blending Ability.* Present the student with single words, in the following sequence:
- Consonant–vowel–consonant (CVC) words
- Words with two-letter blends at the beginning (e.g., *step, slab, plop, crop, blip*)
- Words with ending blends (e.g., *pump, gulp, gust, mint*)
- Words with blends at the beginning and end (e.g., *stump, flint, blast, blunt*)
- Words with three-letter blends (e.g., *strap, scratch, splint*)

For students with strong visual memories, using nonsense words is highly recommended; students must rely on phonetic knowledge to decode nonsense words.

→ ***Knowledge of Syllables.*** It is important to identify whether a student knows what a syllable is. To understand what a syllable is, the student must be able to identify vowels and consonants. First, ask the student to write the alphabet. While the student is writing, take note of letter formations, subvocalizing, automaticity, and whether he or she has to go back to the beginning of the alphabet to recall the next letter. After the student has written the alphabet, ask him or her to circle the vowels. Next, orally present 1-, 2-, 3-, and 4-syllable words and ask the student to clap once for each syllable. Ultimately, you want every student to know that each syllable must contain only one vowel sound. It is important to stress the word *sound* because syllables often have more than one vowel that together make only one sound.

→ ***Knowledge of Syllable Types.*** Once you know that the student understands what a syllable is, it is important to find out whether he or she can identify types of syllables. This knowledge is important because the syllable type dictates the sound that the vowel will make in any given word (e.g., short or long). By asking the student to identify closed and open syllables, you will learn whether the student knows syllable types.

→ ***Knowledge of Syllabication Rules.*** Give examples of multisyllabic words that follow the different syllabication rules and assess whether the student can break up the words adequately to come up with the correct pronunciations. It is best to use unfamiliar words to determine whether the student is decoding or relying on visual memory. The following are some examples of rules:

VC/CV:	gob/lin	**V/CV:**	ba/sic
VC/CCV:	con/trast	**VC/V:**	rap/id
VCC/CCV:	hand/clasp	**V/V:**	tri/ad
VC/CCCV:	con/script		

Determining Whether Naming Speed Is a Problem

Naming speed measures are tests of automaticity. They assess a student's ability to recognize and rapidly retrieve the names of common objects, colors, letters, and numbers. Naming speed measures are brief and easy to use. The student is presented with cards. Each card has several rows of random colors, objects, letters, or numbers. The student is asked to name the items as quickly as possible, starting with the top row and proceeding in left-to-right fashion to the end of the card. The teacher records the total time the student needs to read each card. Teachers can administer a naming speed measure in just minutes. The *Rapid Automatized Naming Test* (Denckla & Rudel, 1976) has been used for many years. It has been renormed and is available from PRO-ED (Wolf & Denckla, 2005). Naming speed measures are also part of the *Comprehensive Test of Phonological Processing* (Wagner, Torgesen, & Rashotte, 1999).

Early identification and prevention of naming speed problems are important. Some students who have difficulty learning to read can capably perform many tasks of phonological awareness but struggle on tasks that assess naming speed. These students may not be identified in traditional screening batteries. Valuable intervention time may be lost as these students continue to struggle with reading for reasons that remain unclear to their parents and teachers.

The Importance of Fluency

Automatic and accurate decoding and word identification skills support reading comprehension. Before students can become fluent readers, they need to become automatic in processes that are critical for reading development. These processes include letter pattern recognition, sound–symbol correspondence, word recognition, and other aspects of reading. For example, many struggling readers acquire decoding skills and begin to recognize common orthographic (letter) patterns; however, their slower learning rate may compromise their rate of reading and ultimately their comprehension of the material. For students to become fluent readers, they need repeated exposure to and practice with reading connected text at their reading level.

Students with phonological processing deficits or naming speed deficits benefit from multisensory reading interventions that emphasize the improvement of their phonological analysis and blending skills and their rate and accuracy of retrieval of common letter patterns (e.g., rime patterns such as "at" or "ine," consonant blends). They also benefit from exercises that expand their vocabulary knowledge. Students with naming speed difficulties further benefit from learning strategies to improve their retrieval skills. These students benefit from intervention programs that emphasize fluency at each level of reading skill development, from letter recognition to word recognition to reading connected text (Donnelly, Miller, & Wolf, 2000).

Although many reading programs include some phonics and decoding instruction, not all include a systematic, multisensory approach. Furthermore, reading and spelling are most often taught as two separate subjects, and connections are often not drawn between them. Spelling rules should be taught in conjunction with decoding skills so that students may more readily see the connections between sound–symbol relationships, reading, spelling, and writing.

∙∙

Determining Whether Spelling Is a Problem

To assess students' spelling problems, give the entire class a diagnostic spelling test that includes words that follow all the different spelling rules and generalizations, as well as sight words. Examine the results of each test to determine which rules or generalizations your students are missing. Directly teach the needed rules (see list in Appendix A.2).

It is important to note that the spelling rules should be taught in a structured, multisensory way. For these rules to be generalized, the students will need extensive practice and application. In addition, it is recommended that the student write rules and generalizations in a strategy notebook so he or she can refer back to them. The teacher can do this writing for students who have difficulty writing (Orton, 1966).

∙∙

Teaching Decoding, Fluency, and Spelling

Decoding

To address decoding difficulties, you need to find out the causes(s) of the student's difficulty. Appendix A.3 is a scope and sequence list for assessing decoding. Students may need instruction beginning at various levels.

➡ *Phonological Awareness.* If weaknesses are present at the phonological awareness level, the student will need remediation from a trained reading specialist or a speech–language pathologist. Helpful approaches include direct, multisensory instruction in these areas:
- *Rhyming activities.* Nursery rhymes, songs, poems, and word play are useful.
- *Elision exercises* (e.g., "Say *stop;* now say it without the /s/"). This activity should be done with both sounds and syllables.
- *Substitution exercises.* For example, set up four different colored blocks to represent the four sounds in a word. Say, "If this says *stop,* make it say *step.*" The student must identify which block made the /o/ sound in *stop,* take it away, and replace it with a block of a different color to represent the new /e/ sound (Lindamood & Lindamood, 1998).

➡ *Sound–Symbol Correspondence.* If weaknesses are present at the sound–symbol correspondence level, the student will need remediation from a trained reading or learning disability specialist. Helpful approaches include the following (Orton, 1966):

- Key words (using one key word per phoneme to cue the student)
- Sand or textured surfaces in the letter's shape so that the child can feel the letter while saying it and hearing it
- Spiraling (mastering one letter before moving to the next, and continually reviewing mastered sounds while introducing new ones)

➡ *Blending.* If weaknesses in blending are present, the student will need remediation from a trained reading specialist. The following approaches are often helpful (Orton, 1966):
- Phonological awareness games
- Direct teaching of blends as blends
- Chunking (grouping by word family)
- Onset and rime patterns
- Finding familiar words within words

➡ *Syllables.* If the student has difficulty knowing which sound the vowel makes within a given word, the student would benefit from instruction about syllable types from a trained reading specialist. Several steps are involved in teaching students about syllables and vowel sounds.

1. Once the student can differentiate between vowels and consonants, you can begin to teach what a syllable is: "A syllable is a word or a part of a word with one vowel sound" (Orton, 1966).

2. Once the student understands what a syllable is and can identify syllables orally, he or she is ready for syllable type instruction.

- *Closed syllable:* a syllable that ends in a consonant, which makes the vowel short (e.g., *hat, strap, stop*)
- *Open syllable:* a syllable that ends in a vowel; the vowel says its name (e.g., *go, she, pro*)
- *Magic* e *syllable:* a syllable that has the vowel–consonant–*e* pattern; the *e* is silent and the medial vowel says its name (e.g., *safe, fine, cute*)
- r-*controlled syllable:* a syllable that has an *r*-controlled vowel in it; the vowel is "bossed around" by the *r* and is neither short nor long (e.g., *start, horn, her*)
- *Diphthong syllable:* a syllable that contains a diphthong (two vowels together that make one sound) (e.g., *boil, scout*)
- –le *syllable:* a syllable with an *le* ending (e.g., sub/tle)
- *Exceptions/word families:* (–ind, –old, –ost, –ild, –ive)

3. If the student has difficulty decoding multisyllabic words, the student would benefit from specific instruction in this area. Because many students exhibit these weaknesses, these skills can

be taught in the classroom, either with the whole class or with a small group. Teach students to look for familiar smaller words or chunks within larger words. Also, teach syllabication rules. Most multisensory, phonetic, systematic approaches recommend that when dividing words, the student should (a) identify all the vowel sounds in the word by placing a V under each one; (b) draw a line or "bridge" connecting the vowel sounds; (c) place a C under all consonants that fall within the "bridge"; and (d) determine which syllable pattern(s) the word contains and break them up appropriately. The following is an example of steps a through d:

a. rabbit	c. rabbit
v v	v c cv
b. rabbit	d. rabbit
v___v	v c:cv

Fluency

Students need frequent opportunities to practice their reading skills with connected text. Struggling readers need many more opportunities to practice than their peers. Teachers can promote fluent reading through their classroom reading instruction in a number of ways.

→ *Repeated Readings.* Rereading of connected text can enhance students' accuracy, speed, and comprehension of printed material. Repeated readings need not be limited to the text level. Many students benefit from practice with word lists or phrases. For students who are struggling readers, teachers can provide modeling of appropriate tone, pace, and intonation while the student follows along with the text. Students can be asked to read the text with a different purpose for each reading.

→ *Reading Programs.* The RAVE-O Program (Donnelly et al., 2000) is an example of a program designed to promote fluent reading skills. This experimental reading program contains numerous suggestions to promote reading fluency by enhancing automatic retrieval of letter patterns and words. The goal is fluent reading of connected text. Suggestions in RAVE-O include the following:
- Providing multiple, multisensory methods for students to practice orthographic pattern recognition and retrieval
- Instructing students in rime families
- Teaching students how to chunk orthographic patterns
- Increasing the depth and breadth of students' vocabulary knowledge

- Teaching morphology of words (e.g., prefixes and suffixes, and how they change meaning)

→ ***Classroom Reading Practices.*** Classroom strategies to improve fluency include *guided reading,* in which the teacher introduces key vocabulary words and concepts and students read as the teacher monitors; *choral reading,* in which the group reads together; and *paired reading,* in which students read aloud to each other. Two recommended programs that include similar strategies are *Great Loops Reading* (Campbell, 1998; Mercer & Campbell, 1998) and *Read Naturally* (Ihnot, 1991).

→ ***Technology.*** Because many students are interested in computers and other technology, these tools can be successfully used to motivate and improve the skills of struggling readers. Children also may benefit from reading along with textbooks on tape. CD-ROM versions of some books are available and may be used to practice reading. There are also computer programs into which teachers can scan material to be read. The student can listen and read silently as the computer reads the text to him or her. The rate of text presentation can be adjusted to accommodate improvements in the child's reading rate.

→ ***Tracking***
1. Using an index card *above* the line helps eliminate the habit of rereading, aids tracking, and can help keep the student's attention.
2. In the middle of a blank transparency, draw two parallel lines the width of the text to be read. Have the student drag the transparency down the page while reading, keeping the text between the two guidelines. This strategy aids tracking while enabling the student to look ahead or at previous text while reading.

→ ***Comprehension and Visualization Strategies.*** If the student is rereading due to comprehension difficulties, the student may benefit from specific comprehension and visualization strategies (see Chapter 4).

Spelling

After assessing students' spelling difficulties (see Appendix A.4), try the following strategies to help students improve their spelling skills.

→ ***Finger Spelling.*** The process of isolating one sound per finger, one syllable at a time, forces the student to attend to individual sounds and to sequence letters (Orton, 1966).

➔ *Air Writing.* Bell (1997) described the process of air writing:
1. Ask students to look up and visualize a blackboard.
2. Have them say the word aloud.
3. Have them say each *letter* (not sound) while writing the letter in the air.
4. Have them read the word aloud again.
5. Ask them questions about the word (e.g., "What is the second letter?").

➔ *Textured Surfaces.* Some students learn better with tactile stimulation.
1. Put sand, sugar, or salt in a paper plate or shallow box.
2. Ask the student to say the word aloud.
3. Have the student say each *letter* (not sound) while writing it in the sand, sugar, or salt.
4. Have the student read the word aloud again.

➔ *Cloze Procedure.* Some students benefit from completing words by gradually filling in more missing letters.
1. Outline the word.
2. Fill in some of the letters, leaving out one letter on the first day.
3. Use the same outlines but leave out two letters on the second day.
4. Use the same outlines but leave out three letters on the third day.
5. On the last day give the student the outline with no letters filled in.
6. Dictate the word with no outline.

Chapter 4

Strategies for Teaching Reading Comprehension

Reading comprehension is the confluence of numerous skills, strategies, and cognitive procedures. In the classroom setting, strong reading comprehension is the underpinning of most content material in the sciences and social sciences. Therefore, teachers need effective strategies for teaching reading comprehension.

What Are the Important Components of Reading Comprehension?

According to Squire (1984), to develop good reading comprehension, students need to learn the following before-, during-, and after-reading skills.

Reading Process	**Before Reading** ⦀ Establish purpose ⦀ Relate text to previous experience ⦀ Look for author's viewpoint

(continues)

Reading Process *Continued.*

During Reading

ⅲ Extract themes and main ideas from text
ⅲ Disregard less relevant details
ⅲ Order details hierarchically
ⅲ Prioritize

After Reading

ⅲ Evaluate content
ⅲ Analyze how effects are achieved
ⅲ Apply independent judgments

Table 4.1 compares students who are skilled readers with students who have reading difficulties.

Helping Students To Develop Effective Reading Strategies

ⅲ **Evaluate your curriculum.** Develop a curriculum that matches the reading level and the needs of your students.
ⅲ **Teach prereading strategies.** These strategies encourage readers to grasp the main themes as a reinforcement for comprehension.
ⅲ **Teach active reading strategies.** These strategies encourage students to be engaged in reading and to read for meaning.
ⅲ **Teach postreading strategies.** These strategies encourage students to reflect, to practice, and to prepare for writing assignments and tests.
ⅲ **Expand students' vocabulary knowledge.** Build students' vocabulary to further enhance their comprehension of reading material.

Evaluate Your Curriculum

To make sure that the *reading level* of classroom material is appropriate for your students, you should do the following:

- Always read and record information from previous evaluations about your students, when it is available.
- Ask parents to complete a questionnaire related to their child's reading habits at home.

TABLE 4.1

A Comparison of Skilled Readers with Students Who Have Difficulties

Skilled readers ...	Students with reading difficulties ...
• move in and out of many reading processes in a recursive manner.	• may become overwhelmed by the many processes interacting during reading.
• know how and when to use specific strategies.	• may have difficulty alternating strategies due to limited flexibility.
• identify which strategies are needed for a particular reading selection.	• may have difficulty selecting appropriate reading strategies at different times.
• monitor and evaluate their use of strategies constantly.	• may not use strategies to help them become actively involved.
• relate new information to what is known throughout the reading process.	• may have limited background knowledge or may have difficulty accessing what they know.
• make predictions and confirm these predictions while reading.	• may not recognize when they have collected sufficient information to form a hypothesis.
• ask themselves questions and recognize main themes.	• may overfocus on details and miss main themes.
• sort through and integrate the many clues provided in the text.	• may have difficulty prioritizing information and sorting through multiple details.
• monitor their level of understanding (e.g., they know when they do not know).	• may struggle to integrate all the information and to monitor their own understanding at the same time.
• make evaluations and judgments about what they read.	• may lack the confidence to develop their own thoughts and opinions.

- Listen to individual students read orally and note their errors. If students mispronounce more than 10% of the words, the text is too difficult.
- Determine readability using a formula such as the Fry readability graph or the Flesch-Kincaid readability procedure (see Appendix A.5).

- Determine whether students are able to answer literal and inferential questions with at least 70% accuracy.

If class texts are too difficult for some students, you might try the following:

- Offer selections on tape.
- Use peer tutoring.
- Copy and enlarge text.
- Find alternative text.
- Ask resource room teacher to assist student(s) with reading the material.

Make sure that *materials* are well structured and have appropriate and understandable language. Before using them with students, do the following:

- Ensure that the main ideas and supporting topics are expressed explicitly throughout each chapter in the text.
- Locate study guides within the text to help focus students on relevant material.
- Highlight and repeat key vocabulary throughout each section.
- Review literature-based materials to be sure that each has a predictable story sequence.

In preparing curriculum-based *lesson plans,* here are some ideas to consider:

- Plan sufficient time to build background knowledge.
- Familiarize students with an author whose work they will read.
- Plan the presentation of content-specific vocabulary.
- Think about the emphasis placed on figurative language in your literature selections and whether to teach the uses of figurative language.
- Plan the strategies you will teach your students for recalling important information.

Teaching Reading Comprehension Strategies

Teaching reading comprehension consists of a number of phases—prereading, active reading, and postreading—and needs to be structured systematically so that the critical components of reading comprehension are addressed. Each phase is discussed in this chapter.

Prereading Phase

<table>
<tr>
<td>

Prereading Strategies

</td>
<td>

▎ Set purposes for reading
▎ Preview vocabulary
▎ Activate prior knowledge
▎ Link known knowledge to new knowledge

</td>
</tr>
</table>

 Set purposes for reading. Setting a purpose for reading encourages your students to become active readers. The following strategies help to establish a purpose for reading:

- Use a K-W-L chart. Make a chart with three columns: Know, Want To Know, and Learned. Under "Know," write information about the topic that the students already know. For the "Want To Know" column, brainstorm a list of information that they might discover through reading. After reading, have students complete the "Learned" column.
- Create a semantic map with information the students already know (see example in Figure 4.1).

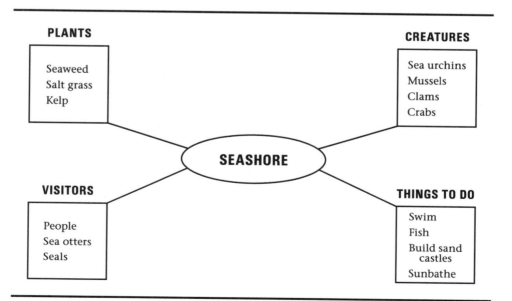

FIGURE 4.1. Semantic map. Before the lesson, students brainstorm knowledge.

Preview text. Teach the students how to preview the text.
- Read and discuss *titles, headings,* and *subheadings.* Consider these questions:
  —What will be the subject of the reading?
  —What important ideas about the subject will students be learning?
  —What do students already know about the subject?
- Study and discuss the book's *cover, illustrations, charts,* and *maps.*
  —What does the cover of the book suggest to the reader?
  —How do charts and other visuals support the information in the text?
- Create a *prereading story map.* Present to students the key story components in a semantic map (see example in Figure 4.2). After the students read the title and first chapter, they add components to the story map. Students might try to make predictions using the story map. As students continue to read the story, the map is amended at critical points as original predictions are confirmed and new predictions are made (Indrisano, 1984).

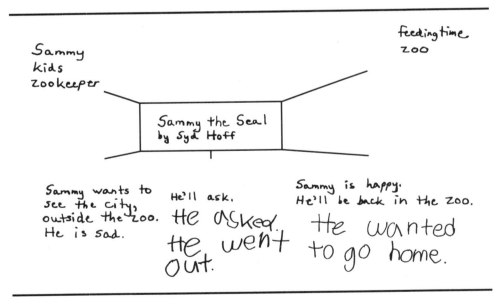

FIGURE 4.2. Example of a story map.

 Preview vocabulary. Read and discuss *key words* from each section of the text.
- Have students write words on index cards.
- Have students use words in sentences.
- Do a *concept sort* with the vocabulary words: (a) Distribute cards with the vocabulary words taken from the reading.

(b) Have the students sort the words into categories or have them create their own categories. (c) After the words are sorted, organize a discussion as to how the vocabulary words relate to the reading.

- Illustrate key words or major concepts.
- Locate pictorial examples of key words in magazines or on the Internet.

➡ *Activate prior knowledge.* Various techniques can be used to activate students' previous knowledge.

- Provide key concepts from the passage to be read.
- Have students generate words and ideas related to the concepts.
- Record students' ideas on the board in the form of a web.
- Create a semantic map (refer to Figure 4.1). (a) As students brainstorm ideas from class discussions, words are grouped in categories and a master map is created. (b) The teacher can add his or her words to the map at any time. (c) The interrelationships among the words are discussed, including similarities and differences. (d) After reading, new concepts can be added to the semantic map (see Figure 4.3).

Active Reading Phase

<table>
<tr>
<td>

Fiction Reading Strategies

</td>
<td>

▥ Create mental images
▥ Complete story maps
▥ Create episode webs
▥ Use Post-it notes
▥ Teach self-questioning strategies
▥ Use highlighting for literature

</td>
</tr>
</table>

© 2006 by PRO-ED, Inc.

<table>
<tr>
<td>

Nonfiction Reading Strategies

</td>
<td>

▥ Use "Skim, RAP, and Map"
▥ Highlight text
▥ Make margin notes
▥ Use semantic mapping
▥ Create expository maps
▥ Make outlines
▥ Use Triple Note Tote strategy

</td>
</tr>
</table>

© 2006 by PRO-ED, Inc.

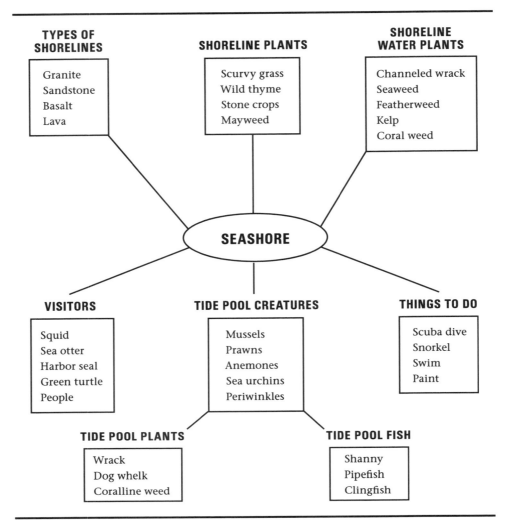

FIGURE 4.3. Semantic map with new concepts added after the lesson.

Active Reading Strategies for Fiction

 Create mental images. Many good readers make sense of text by forming mental images as they read. Imagery improves comprehension and memory by linking words with visual images and integrating parts of the text with the whole. Students with learning difficulties, particularly those with language-based difficulties, may not automatically visualize as they read, but can develop this strategy through systematic instruction. Ironically, many students may read text fluently and accurately, but remember very little of what they read. Even when students remember facts, some are unable to relate these facts to the main ideas. These students may spend many hours rereading text, yet their performance and grades do not reflect the level of their effort.

As early as first grade, teachers can help children to learn to visualize and comprehend language. One effective curriculum specifically designed to teach students to create mental images is *Visualizing and Verbalizing* (Bell, 1991a, 1991b). Most approaches for improving visualization incorporate the following steps:

1. *Start visualization training with familiar words or experiences.* Instruct students to mentally "make a picture" or "make a movie." Ask specific questions to elicit detailed images (e.g., color, size, shape).

2. *Introduce short, concrete, descriptive passages at levels below students' grade placement.* Read these passages to students. As students develop proficiency, gradually add oral reading, then silent reading. Later, increase the length of the text and vary the subject matter.

3. *Use questioning to help students form images after each sentence.* Questions should focus on attributes of the images (e.g., color, size) and serve to increase the number of details within the images. Gradually extend the length of text and discuss images after each paragraph, then after each page.

4. *Present model images and discuss these.* When presenting models, act as an active participant (e.g., "In my movie [picture] I saw …").

5. *Rehearse the visual sequence.* In the Wilson Reading System (Wilson, 1988), students are instructed to "Rewind the film and watch it again." In *Visualizing and Verbalizing* (Bell, 1991a), students create a sentence-by-sentence picture by describing, "Here I saw …" for each sentence and then for each paragraph.

6. *Formulate a verbal summary.* The verbal summary should reflect an understanding of the main themes, and how individual parts relate to the whole.

➡ *Complete story maps.* Major story elements include the setting, characters, plot, and resolution. One typical story map is shown in Figure 4.2. Another approach to story mapping, which entails using a structured, multisensory approach to reading comprehension, is available as part of the Project Read Story Form curriculum (Greene & Enfield, 1999).

➡ *Create episode webs.* In episode webs, the reader summarizes each section of a story that is structured by a series of loosely related episodes (see Figure 4.4).

➡ *Use Post-it notes.* Students who are unable to write in their books or who have difficulty locating key pages may find Post-it notes helpful.
- When reading novels, students can summarize each chapter on a Post-it note, indicating major events, changes in setting,

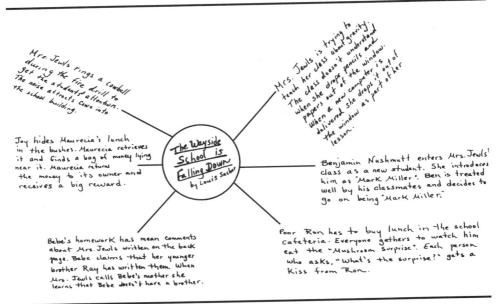

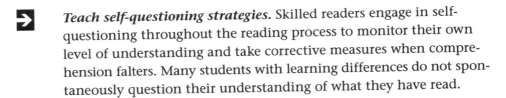

FIGURE 4.4. Example of an episode web. Summaries for episodes are placed at each leg.

new characters, symbolism, and thematic developments. When the students need to write summaries or book reports, they can take these Post-it notes and arrange them on a blank sheet or on acetate sleeves.

- Students can use Post-it notes to give a completed chapter a new title, followed by a brief explanation of how that title fits the chapter.

→ ***Teach self-questioning strategies.*** Skilled readers engage in self-questioning throughout the reading process to monitor their own level of understanding and take corrective measures when comprehension falters. Many students with learning differences do not spontaneously question their understanding of what they have read.

Principles of Self-Questioning

1. Students are taught how to generate questions and how to locate main ideas.
2. Teachers model their own internal dialogue for students, and students practice these dialogues.
3. Questions may assess the students' understanding about sections they have already read or may allow them to predict what is likely to occur.
4. Teachers model main idea questions, which students paraphrase. Detail questions that can be lifted from the text verbatim are discouraged.

5. Questions should require students to reflect on the purpose of the passage and encourage them to make informed predictions.

➡ *Use highlighting for literature.* Students should be encouraged to highlight, in their personal books, words and phrases that name or describe the setting, characters, conflict(s), climax, and resolution. Using a color-coded key, have students use different colored markers to highlight separate features (e.g., blue for setting, green for character).

Active Reading Strategies for Nonfiction

➡ *Use "Skim, RAP, and Map"* (developed by Taber, Institute for Learning and Development).
1. *Skim* the text by reading titles, headings, and subheadings; captions under pictures; charts; maps; initial sentence in each paragraph; last sentence of final paragraph; words in quotes, italics, or bold type; questions embedded in the text; introductions and summaries.
2. *RAP* (**R**ead, **A**sk questions, **P**araphrase). For each section, form a question from the heading or topic sentence, locate the answer, and paraphrase it.
3. *Map* by creating a two-column chart (divide page down the center). Place RAP questions in the left-hand column, and list answers in the corresponding right-hand column. The two-column format also allows students to self-quiz when they study.

➡ *Highlight text.* Beginning with simple text, teach students, when using their personal books, to look for, find, and highlight the subject of the text, the topic sentence, ideas that support the topic, and key vocabulary. Students can use color coding (e.g., blue to identify the subject, yellow for the topic sentence, and red for supporting ideas) to mark the text and enhance their comprehension.

➡ *Make margin notes.* As students begin to read on their own, they should begin to use margin notes in their personal books and notebooks. This activity encourages active learning, thoughtful reading, and self-monitoring.
✓ Check mark confirms understanding.
? Question mark indicates confusion.
! Exclamation point indicates amazement.
Simple cartoons may be used to summarize the main idea.

➜ *Use semantic mapping.* Semantic mapping, a visual presentation that links verbal concepts, helps students to
- Focus on central themes and key vocabulary to "see" how they interrelate
- Focus on the structure of the text
- Learn that specific types of literature have a similar structure
- Learn the structure of expository writing
- Learn how to prioritize information, organize language, focus on relevant themes, and improve comprehension

➜ *Create expository maps.* The organization of factual texts is based on the concepts presented. An expository map is an excellent way to activate prior knowledge and to introduce new concepts (see Figure 4.5). These maps can be used in a postreading activity as a way of adding or modifying material based on new information acquired through reading.

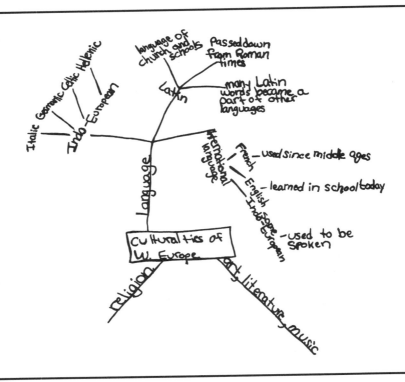

FIGURE 4.5. Example of an expository map.

➜ *Make outlines.* As students begin to read more expository text as part of their curriculum, they need to learn how to collect, organize, and synthesize the information. They need to understand how the information presented in expository text is related to the topic. One curriculum that uses a multisensory, systematic approach to reading comprehension is the *Project Read: Report Form Comprehension Guide* developed by Project Read (Greene & Enfield, 1999). This guidebook presents strategies for identifying the subject of an article, "unlocking the key facts," and selecting the supporting details. With these strategies, the student can focus on the relevant material that needs to be learned for a test or used in writing a report.

➜ *Use the Triple Note Tote strategy* (BrainCogs, Institute for Learning and Development/ResearchILD & FableVision, 2001). This strategy consists of a three-column note-taking format. The student writes questions or terms in the first column, answers or definitions in the second column, and a remembering strategy, such as an acronym or a picture, in the last column.

Postreading Phase

Postreading Strategies	‖ Use question–answer activities ‖ Develop summaries ‖ Create outlines ‖ Use writing activities ‖ Organize group discussions ‖ Develop related learning experiences

© 2006 by PRO-ED, Inc.

Use question–answer activities. Every part of the curriculum that requires reading is followed by a question–answer component to check for understanding. The teacher's goal is to create question–answer activities that enhance the students' understanding of the material.

1. *Asking questions about stories* (Grades 1–3). Develop specific questions for each story based on features common to all stories:
- *Where* and *when* does the story take place? (setting)
- *Who* are the main characters? (protagonists)
- *What* is the problem? (problem)
- *Why* is this happening? (goal)
- *How* is the problem resolved? (resolution)

Initially these questions can be answered by filling in the blanks. As students become more familiar with the structure, questions can be answered in short answers.

Key words (e.g., *setting, protagonist*) also can be taught using a visual strategy, such as the Star strategy (described in Chapter 5). The

Star Strategy can be used flexibly during elementary, middle, and high school.

2. *Answering questions from expository text* (Grades 4–12). Use Bloom's (1956) Taxonomy to develop questions related to each level of learning:

Bloom's Taxonomy
- Knowledge (e.g., explain, list)
- Comprehension (e.g., summarize, paraphrase)
- Analysis (e.g., compare, contrast)
- Synthesis (e.g., add new ideas, identify additional research)
- Evaluation (e.g., form opinions, make judgments)
- Self-Questioning (e.g., turn headings and subheadings into questions and review the material)

After modeling appropriate questions with students, have them develop questions and share these with classmates. These questions can be the basis for group discussion.

3. *The 3H strategy* (Grades 5–6). Teach students to use various "helpers," such as the 3H strategy, each time they answer a question from text (Graham & Wong, 1993).
- How will I answer this question?
- Where can I find the answer to this question?
  Here: Use information found in one sentence in the passage.
  Hidden: Use more than one idea from the passage to answer.
  In my *Head:* Use what I already know.

→ *Develop summaries.* Summarizing is an important technique that many students find challenging and therefore tend not to use.

1. *Semantic maps and summary maps.* Create a "map" that highlights the main themes of a story. A story map has the title in the middle with four to six main ideas from the reading listed in a circle around the title. Similarly, a summary map for expository writing has the main idea in the middle with the supporting details in a circle around the main idea. The Star strategy also can be used to help students visualize the key information (see Chapter 5).

2. *Use summary rules.* When summarizing stories, students should learn to use rules such as the following:
- Delete trivial information, or any information that does not support the topic.
- Delete redundant information, or information that is repeated several times.

- Include answers to who, what, when, where, how, and why questions.

Create outlines. Outlining is an important skill for summarizing text.
- Use the *title* of the chapter for the title of the outline.
- Use the *headings* for the subjects of the outline, labeled with Roman numerals.
- Use the *subheadings* from the text for the main ideas of the outline, labeled with capital letters.
- Use *sentences and phrases* from the paragraphs for supporting details, labeled with Arabic numerals.

Use writing activities. When students write about what they have read, they are forced to process the information more thoroughly and more actively. Thus, they develop a deeper understanding of the reading material.

Writing Activities for Fiction

◆ *Summary logs.* Students should write entries in a summary log at the end of each chapter. A student might include impressions of characters, the introduction of new characters, or predictions. The teacher can either provide specific guidelines for each entry or allow the student to decide what to include in the entry. Summary logs have the following benefits:

1. They reinforce the concept that all stories have a similar skeleton, which includes setting, characters, conflict, climax, and resolution.
2. They are helpful for students who have difficulty keeping track of characters and events.
3. They can be used as a reference for writing book reports.

◆ *Reaction logs.* Students maintain a journal with their reactions to and comments concerning characters and events in the story.

◆ *Literature logs.* Students keep a record of the pages they have read and comments about the reading. Students discuss their feelings about a character or event and whether they can relate these to their own experiences. Students can also predict different outcomes.

◆ *Dialogue journals.* Through journal writing, students discuss their books and the strategies they use while reading. The teacher responds to the students by writing comments that help them to further explore their thoughts (see Figure 4.6). Students can be encouraged to focus on strategies (e.g., making predictions, requesting clarification, evaluating the text). They can also be encouraged to comment on literary elements such as leads, genre, themes, figurative language, and author's style (Atwell, 1987).

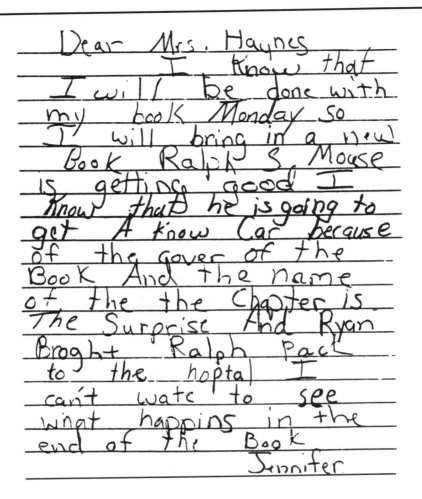

Dear Mrs. Haynes
        I know that
I will be done with
my book Monday so
I will bring in a new
Book Ralph S Mouse
is getting good I
know that he is going to
get A know Car because
of the Cover of the
Book And the name
of the the Chapter is
The Surprise And Ryan
Broght Ralph Pack
to the hoptal I
can't wate to see
what happins in the
end of the Book
                    Jennifer

October 27, 1999

Dear Jennifer,
    You are showing me another
strategy that you have learned. Readers
predict what they think will happen
next. You have predicted what will
happen to Ralph S Mouse at the end
of the book. Let me know if your
prediction is correct in your next
letter. Please remember your date.
                    Mrs. Haynes

FIGURE 4.6. Example of a dialogue journal.

◆ *Book reports.* Before reading begins, the teacher does the following:

1. Determine which strategies students will need to know.
2. Decide on the focus of the report.
3. Tell students what the report should be about, so they can prepare for the activity as they read (e.g., if they will be writing a character description, the students can be gathering information on the characters as they read the story).
4. Teach prereading and active reading strategies that are relevant to the focus of the book report.
5. Consider assigning different formats (e.g., newspaper review, cartoons, locating textual evidence that supports the title).

◆ *New ending.* Students can alter some of the facts of a particular text and rewrite the ending. Alternatively, they can write a prologue or epilogue.

◆ *Alternate viewpoint.* Students can rewrite a chapter from another character's viewpoint. Letters or journal entries can also be written from the point of view of different characters.

◆ *Original story.* Have students write original stories. First they should outline their stories using a story map. Have the students enter original characters, settings, and plot summaries on the story map before writing their stories.

➜ ## Writing Activities for Nonfiction

◆ *Learning logs.* After reading in the content areas, students record new concepts they have learned. In Grades 1 through 3, students select a few new facts, write a sentence for each fact, and then illustrate. In Grades 4 through 8, students write a paragraph about the concepts, and draw diagrams or charts to illustrate. They can also develop questions from subheadings and relate their paragraphs to these questions.

◆ *Newspaper articles.* Students use facts from their reading to develop newspaper articles that explore the issues from a particular angle. Students may benefit from using a list of *wh–* questions (who, what, when, where, why, how).

◆ *Interviews.* Students create mock interviews with famous people from their reading, and use information from the text as the basis for their questions and answers. Students might even conduct actual interviews with people who are knowledgeable about a subject that is being studied in the text.

◆ *Persuasive essays.* Students use facts from their reading to support a particular viewpoint. Provide models of persuasive essays to illustrate a structure that the students can follow.

◆ *Research papers.* Students organize and consolidate the information from several sources into research papers. (Suggestions regarding structured processes for research papers are provided in Chapter 7).

➜ ***Organize group discussions.*** A group discussion is not a question-and-answer session, but a *dialogue* between students and teacher. Students learn to participate through teacher modeling. Discussions help students recognize that their thoughts are valued, because they do not feel they are being tested. Competition is reduced, and even reticent students feel that it is safe to participate.

➜ ***Develop related learning experiences.*** Various learning experiences related to the themes in a text can be used to extend the students' understanding of concepts. These can include films, Internet sources (e.g., a virtual tour of a region of the world), field trips, demonstrations, discussions, lectures, and additional readings. This new information can be linked to the reading by adding information to a story map, outline, or matrix.

◆ *Compare and contrast map.* Students compare and contrast sources of information on a Venn diagram (see Appendix B.1). For example, the events in a particular book can be contrasted with the movie version.

◆ *Compare and contrast matrix.* After reading and/or viewing several presentations of the same theme, students compare and contrast the versions using a chart similar to that shown in Figure 4.7.

◆ *Related projects.* Projects can reinforce concepts and enhance students' understanding of material. The teacher may want to allow students to choose a method of presentation that capitalizes on their strengths. The following are some possibilities:

Models, maps, and dioramas
Timelines, cartoon strips, and videotapes
Travel brochures, photographs, drawings, and posters
Role-plays, debates, and oral presentations
Student-made board games

◆ *Plot profiles.* Students summarize and evaluate the plot of a well-structured story (Butler, 1988):

1. In small groups, students summarize the main events of the story.
2. They list main events in sequence on a chart.
3. Students collectively discuss the level of excitement they felt for each event and rate each on a 10-point scale.
4. Students plot points on a graph to illustrate their reactions using a plot profile (see Figure 4.8).

	Version 1	Version 2	Version 3	Alike	Different	Conclusions
Title	"The Little Boy's Secret"	"The Giant Who Threw Tantrums"	"The Giant Who Was Afraid of Butterflies"			
Setting	woods and giant's castle	village and woods	valley and hill	Each story takes place "long ago."		Stories take place where there is a lot of space for giants to roam.
Characters	Little boy, 3 nasty giants	Little boy, kind giant, foolish villagers	Little boy, friendly giant, mean witch	In 2 and 3, boy and giant are friends.	The bad guy is different in each one.	Sometimes unlikely friendships can occur.
Problem	The boy is kidnapped by giants because he won't tell his secret.	The giant throws tantrums because he can't whistle.	The witch puts spell on the giant.		In each of the stories the conflict is caused by different characters.	Where there are giants and witches you can expect trouble!
Events	The boy tells each giant his secret and they run away frightened.	The villagers hear noises but don't believe they are caused by a giant, even when the boy sees the giant.	The witch casts a spell and the giant sees things as twice his size. The boy gets the giant eyeglasses, which return his sight to normal.			In each story the boy is much wiser than the giant.
Ending	The boy breaks out in measles, revealing his secret.	The boy teaches the giant to whistle. Now the villagers hear whistling off in the distance.	The giant and boy scold the witch and go off to play.			Ongoing friendships between boys and giants are rare.

FIGURE 4.7. Compare and contrast matrix for three stories. Stories compiled from *The Book of Giant Stories* by Harrison, 1972, New York: American Heritage Press.

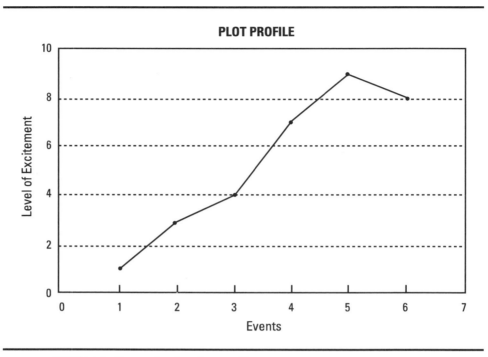

FIGURE 4.8. Example of a plot profile.

Expand Vocabulary Knowledge

Expand Vocabulary Knowledge	‖ Teach vocabulary words directly. ‖ Teach strategies for analyzing word meanings through context. ‖ Teach strategies for analyzing word meanings through structure. ‖ Teach VOCAB-LIT strategy.

 Teach vocabulary words directly. Research has shown that students with weaknesses in reading know fewer words than their more skilled peers. Direct methods of instruction have been shown to be effective in improving the quality of vocabulary knowledge for both skilled and less skilled readers (Chall, 1987; Curtis, 1986, 1987). Students with learning difficulties remember new vocabulary best when using methods that use mnemonic (memory) aids and when they can relate new vocabulary to prior knowledge (Mastropieri, Scruggs, & Levin, 1985; Roswell & Natchez, 1977).

◆ *Key word method.* The key word method incorporates the following principles:

- *Recording.* Students choose a key word that sounds similar to the target word.
- *Relating.* The recorded word is related to the target word's meaning through a picture.
- *Retrieving.* Students think of the picture, associate this image with the key word, and remember the target word.

Students' key words and interactive pictures can be recorded on index cards and added to individual word banks. Sentences that contain both the target word and the key word can be developed to further illustrate the definition. For example, a high school senior developed a key word for the word *belligerence* (see Figure 4.9).

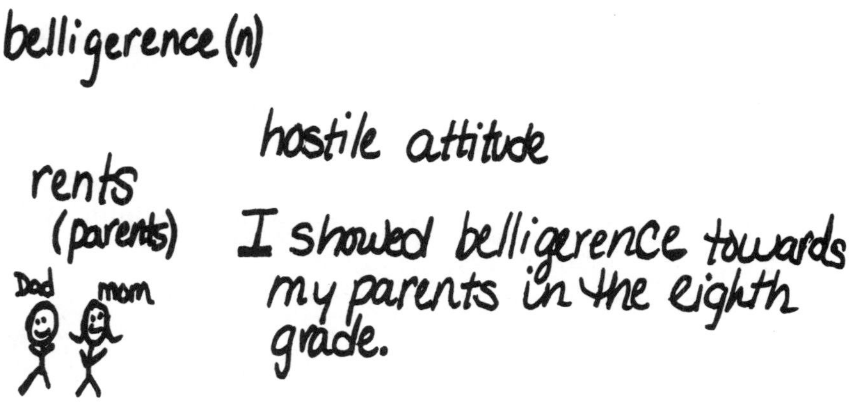

FIGURE 4.9. Mnemonic strategy for recalling terminology and concepts: key word for the word *belligerence.*

◆ *Word wheels.* Develop a synonym, antonym, or homonym web. In the center of an index card or page, place the main vocabulary word inside a bubble. Place related synonyms, antonyms, or homonyms around the bubbles, and connect them to the main word with "spokes."

◆ *Concept sort.* A concept sort can be used as a pre- or postreading activity, with either literature or expository material. Students can work in pairs, in groups, or individually. The teacher writes vocabulary words from the reading on note cards. Students sort words into categories that teachers provide, or students create their own categories. After the words are sorted, the class discussion focuses on the links between the vocabulary words and the text.

◆ *Multiple meanings.* The concept that words can have more than one meaning can be introduced as early as first grade. For students with learning differences, this concept needs to be continually reinforced through various tasks. When you and your students are reading through a list of spelling words, discuss with students words that have more than one meaning. With younger students, you can use pictures to illustrate the different meanings. Older students can write down at least two different ways the word might be used, as done here for *fly* and *cross.*

1. He caught a *fly* ball when he played centerfield in Tuesday's game.
2. A *fly* landed on the cow's tail.

1. Look both ways before you *cross* the street.
2. Her mother was very *cross* when Judy did not come home on time.

◆ *Semantic feature analysis.* Words that share certain features are selected from the reading lesson. These are listed in a column on a chalkboard or a piece of paper. Students generate features that are contained in at least one of the words. These features are listed in a row across the top of the board to form a matrix. This is called a *matrix splash.* Students assign plus or minus values to words and features (see Figure 4.10). As students become more proficient, scales of numbers could replace plus and minus values

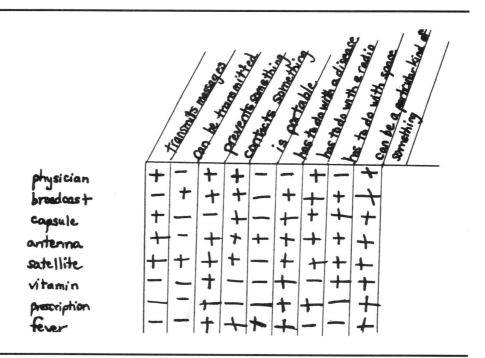

FIGURE 4.10. A vocabulary grid illustrating semantic feature analysis.

to indicate varying degrees of features. Students can continue to add more words and features to the grid. Through discussion, students discover the uniqueness of words, as they see that no two words have the same pattern of pluses and minuses.

➡ *Teach strategies for analyzing word meanings through context.* Skilled readers develop most of their vocabulary knowledge through reading connected text (Nagy, Herman, & Anderson, 1985). Students with learning and attention difficulties often read less than their skilled peers, and may lack sufficient exposure to words in context. They often have difficulty inferring word meaning through context. To maximize their reading experience, they can develop strategies for using context to learn word meanings.

Effective Strategies for Using Context To Learn Word Meanings

- Provide passages that contain the words in a variety of contexts or develop a list of 7 to 10 sentences that provide clues to the meaning of each word.
- Use various cues to infer meanings of the words, including category membership, physical properties of the word, and the importance of the word's meaning to understanding the text.
- Provide opportunities for students to write the words in their own contexts.
- Record unknown words on index cards along with the sentences in which they were found and their possible definitions. The words can be added to individual word banks.

© 2005 by PRO-ED, Inc.

➡ *Teach strategies for analyzing word meanings through structure.* An excellent way to teach word meaning is through word structure— that is, the meanings of roots, prefixes, and suffixes, and the effect that affixes have on the meanings of words.

◆ *Structural methods for elementary students.* Teach elementary students the following: (a) what prefixes and suffixes are, (b) how they can change the meanings of words, and (c) how prefixes and suffixes affect the word's usage in a sentence.

1. Begin with the most commonly used prefixes and suffixes.

Prefixes	Suffixes
un–	–ing
re–	–ed
pre–	–s and –es
in–	–tion

2. Write each affix on an index card, with its meaning(s) on the back of the card.
3. Attach affixes to root words and have students highlight affixes.
4. Create sentences using words with attached affixes underlined, and have students define the words.
5. Have students use words in their own sentences.

◆ *Structural methods for secondary students.*

- Teach affixes and roots that carry clear, consistent meaning; occur frequently; and can be used to identify the words' meanings (e.g., *un–, –able, dis–*). Select specific affixes and roots depending on the needs of the learner. Determine whether students need to learn non-English roots, and decide which roots are appropriate to teach based on reading demands and student goals.
- Teach meanings of affixes and roots by using words that are already in the students' vocabulary (e.g., teach *–cracy* through *democracy,* then add a new word *theocracy*). Have students develop an ongoing vocabulary file. Create a holistic understanding of each new word by including the part of speech, a mnemonic aid, and a descriptive sentence using the word and, if possible, its meaning or a partial clue.

➡ ***Teach VOCAB-LIT strategy (high school).*** Following a reading assignment, VOCAB-LIT reinforces concepts in the text and extends students' vocabulary knowledge (Chase & Duffelmeyer, 1990). The procedure follows:
1. The teacher chooses a word that is conceptually important to the major themes in the text.
2. Using the form shown in Figure 4.11, students individually indicate their familiarity with the word.
3. As a group, students share prior knowledge of the word.
4. On the form, students copy the sentence from the text in which the word occurred.
5. The group discusses the meaning of the word based on this context.
6. Students locate the word in the dictionary and copy the appropriate definition.
7. Students discuss how knowledge of the word has enhanced their understanding of the text.
8. Each student is assigned a word to present to the group from the previous day's reading assignment.

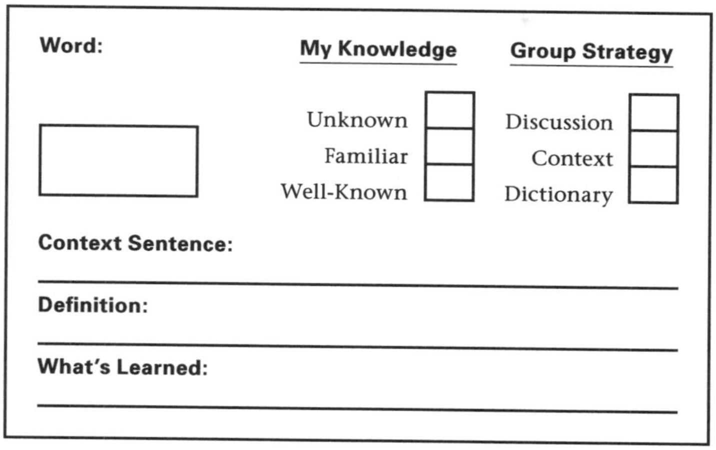

Word:	My Knowledge	Group Strategy
	Unknown ☐	Discussion ☐
	Familiar ☐	Context ☐
	Well-Known ☐	Dictionary ☐

Context Sentence:

Definition:

What's Learned:

FIGURE 4.11. Example of a VOCAB-LIT card.

Overview

Consider the following questions before planning reading comprehension instruction:

- What processes does this particular task require?
- What strategies do I need to teach all students based on the demands of this task?
- What modifications do I need to make for individual students who may need additional support?
- How can you use reading comprehension strategies during a reading lesson?

Imagine that you are a fourth-grade teacher working with a literature group. You have eight students in your group, three of whom have learning difficulties. You have chosen the text *Trouble River* by Betsy Byars (1989), because it is fast paced and uses understandable language. This is a story about a pioneer boy and his grandmother who vacate their cabin to escape hostile Indians. Their only chance for survival is to travel downstream on a raft to join the boy's parents in a neighboring town. Your activities may be similar to those shown in Table 4.2.

During this unit, each student has developed a unique repertoire of active reading strategies. Students may have reached different levels of understanding of the book and their reading comprehension has proceeded at different paces and in manners conducive to each student's learning style.

(text continues on p. 68)

TABLE 4.2

How Instruction Can Be Individualized To Promote Reading Comprehension

Group	Students with Reading Comprehension Difficulties		
	Sara	Bill	Tom
Eight students; heterogeneous, flexible groups; focus on reading comprehension, action/adventure genre, sequential organization	LD; processing skills are strong in visual channel, weak in language	LD; good comprehender, poor decoder	ADD; overfocuses on details
Activate Students' Prior Knowledge			
Discuss early pioneers and the dangers they encountered.	Provide pictures of early pioneers. Speak slowly. Allow extra time to process information and responses.	Assume he will follow general discussion.	Provide preferential seating. Make frequent eye contact. Provide pictures of early pioneers.
Review Vocabulary			
Present words in sentences that have many context clues. Students write possible definitions for the words. Students volunteer definitions, which are recorded on a class chart.	Discussion of how to use context clues is critical to Sara's understanding of this strategy.	Assist with word identification. Bill should syllabicate and decode words. Use these words in Bill's decoding and spelling lessons.	Check that Tom has grasped the directions and remains on task.
Reciprocal Teaching			
Read first few pages silently as a group to identify major characters, setting, basic problem in plot. plot. Change group leaders at natural break points.			Have Tom mark predetermined break points.

(continues)

TABLE 4.2 *Continued.*

How Instruction Can Be Individualized To Promote Reading Comprehension

Group	Students with Reading Comprehension Difficulties		
	Sara	**Bill**	**Tom**
Reciprocal Teaching (*continued*) Facilitate and model appropriate strategy use.			
Semantic Mapping Use a variation of the story map to accommodate the episodic subplots that occur.	The visual representation of the map is critical for Sara. Rephrase questions about the setting, such as "At what time?" and "In what place?" because Sara often confuses *where* and *when*.		
Silent Reading Provide quiet time for sections of the story to be read silently. Students record reactions in literature logs and bring to group discussions.		Pair Bill and Tom to read orally in a quiet section of the room. Each assumes the responsibility of "tutoring" the other. Tom assists Bill with decoding difficult, multisyllabic words.	Bill helps Tom remain on task.
Group Discussion Make and confirm predictions using the map. Discusss students' reactions from logs, including those regarding strategy use.	Allow extra time to process information and formulate responses.		Mapping is critical for Tom, who has difficulty prioritizing details and identifying main themes.

(continues)

TABLE 4.2 *Continued.*
How Instruction Can Be Individualized To Promote Reading Comprehension

| Group | Students with Reading Comprehension Difficulties | | |
	Sara	Bill	Tom
Group Discussion (*continued*)			
Amend vocabulary chart to reflect increased understanding of the words as they are encountered in text. Add words to individual word banks.	Group discussion is critical for Sara to learn word meanings as well as to learn strategies for unlocking word meanings through context.		
Plot Profile			
After story is completed, students analyze how subplots relate to the larger plot. Help students make judgments and negotiate responses.	Profile provides visual representation of plot. Sara develops understanding of sequence.	Profile helps Bill to develop part–whole relationships.	Profile helps Tom to prioritize details and to integrate these with the main theme.

Conclusion

Meeting the wide range of reading needs within a heterogeneous classroom is a major challenge. The beauty of adopting a strategic approach to teaching reading comprehension is that many of the recommended activities benefit all students, not only those with learning difficulties. Remember, change is gradual. Think big, but start small. Select a new strategy and incorporate this into a series of lessons. When you know that the students are comfortable with this strategy and you can see that they are using it, try something new.

Chapter 5

Strategies for Enhancing Written Language

It was the style of teaching that was not working, not my mind.

—Kira, 11th grader

In this chapter we discuss the important components of written language and ways you can help your students become better writers. Providing a variety of writing strategies at each stage of the writing process will ensure that all students become successful writers.

Helping Students To Become Better Writers	
	▥ Help your students to develop and practice effective writing strategies.
	▥ Help students to internalize strategies so these can be used automatically.
	▥ Provide constant practice and spiraling.
	▥ Have students practice writing by submitting multiple drafts.

(continues)

Helping Students To Become Better Writers *Continued.*	▥ Ensure that students understand the importance of the different stages of writing. ▥ Remember that, compared with their peers, students with learning difficulties need more review, practice, repetition, and success to use these strategies independently.

Why Teach Strategies in Writing?

Writing instruction historically has focused on the final products of writing. Teachers frequently assigned topics, graded papers, made corrections, and returned these to students. The belief was that students would internalize the teacher's comments (if they read them at all) and generalize these to the next composition. In addition, exercises in grammar were completed and graded; the belief was that students would learn *how* to write simply by learning *what* a sentence comprised.

In the past, little class time was devoted to teaching students the process of writing. Handwriting, spelling, and sentence structure received most of the attention in writing instruction, whereas little attention was given to teaching higher level thought processes, including planning, revising, and self-monitoring (or self-regulation). These processes, however, are important components of writing.

According to Squire (1984), the writing process requires students to learn before-, during-, and after-writing skills.

Before Writing
- Set goals
- Generate ideas (e.g., brainstorm)
- Consider audience
- Determine point of view
- Identify main themes
- Organize ideas in a logical sequence

During Writing
- Prioritize
- Select appropriate language to match thought
- Apply strategies flexibly
- Coordinate multiple subskills and processess

After Writing
- Evaluate
- Revise

- Edit
- Apply outside standards of correctness

Skilled writers move in and out of these stages spontaneously rather than following them in a linear fashion. For example, editing for spelling or punctuation errors may occur while writing; however, when writing is complete, editing may occur again using a more systematic approach (see Table 5.1).

Teaching Writing Strategies

You can help your students develop writing strategies in the following ways:

- Develop specific goals for each writing assignment. Tailor goals to individual students' needs.
- Directly teach prewriting strategies such as brainstorming and organizing.
- Directly teach writing at the sentence, paragraph, and multi-paragraph levels.
- Teach self-regulation strategies such as revising and editing.
- Use appropriate technology.
- Tie assessment of writing to expectations.

Develop Specific Goals for Each Writing Assignment

 Establish a purpose for writing. The teacher, or the teacher and students together, set goals for the paper and list these goals. It is useful to consider the following points (adapted from Harris & Graham, 1992):

- What is the general purpose of the paper? (to inform, to entertain, to persuade, to compare/contrast, to retell)
- What is the general structure of the paper? (story format, main ideas and details, comparison/contrast)
- Where can students find sources of information? (personal experience, background knowledge, interviews, class lecture, textbooks, additional research)
- What are the expectations regarding specific writing skills?
- Which writing components will be emphasized? (vocabulary, sentence structure, spelling, handwriting, capitalization and punctuation)
- What are the expectations regarding length, format, and due dates?

TABLE 5.1

Writing Strategies of Skilled Writers and Students with Writing Difficulties

Skilled Writers	Students with Writing Difficulties
Understand the depth and creativity inherent in good writing	Overfocus on the mechanical details; understand writing only as a process of constructing sentences, using correct punctuation and spelling
Plan an approach, either explicitly or implicitly	Often begin writing without any planning, just to get it over with
Formulate main themes and develop these with supportive details	May have difficulty identifying main themes; may have difficulty staying with the topic; may provide few details
Organize ideas in a logical sequence	May have limited understanding of the organization of text structures; often write ideas in random order
Write and revise their ideas	Display limited writing fluency; are reluctant to revise ideas
Edit for spelling, capitalization, and punctuation	May not easily recognize their errors; may not know how to correct errors
Monitor their thought processes; devise solutions to problems they encounter	May be unaware of the strategies they are using or the strategies they need
Demonstrate proficiency in numerous subskills and processes for writing including those related to motor demands (letter formation, fluency, spatial organization), form (sentence structure, syntax, punctuation, spelling), and content (vocabulary, organization)	May have weaknesses in subskills that can impede their performance on higher level components of the writing process; may have trouble integrating numerous subskills and shifting strategies when needed
Often apply what they have learned from reading as they write (e.g., genre, language usage, sentence structures)	Often avoid reading for leisure and do not generalize principles to writing

Establish objectives. At each grade level, students should practice different forms of writing, including fictional, narrative, procedural, persuasive, and descriptive. The specific objectives for each assignment can be adjusted to meet the needs of various students, especially those with learning difficulties. Teachers create objectives for each writing assignment to meet the requirements of the curriculum and to make the writing process meaningful. Objectives can be clearly communicated to students through the use of performance criteria, rubrics, or Focused Correction Areas (Collins, 1992). Assessment of student writing should be directly related to specific objectives set by the teacher and previously communicated to the student.

◆ *Performance criteria.* Students benefit from having a clear understanding of the objectives of the assignment before they begin writing. One method of devising and communicating clear goals for writing is a list of performance criteria. Specific objectives are given point values, which clearly communicate to the student the elements of writing that are the focus for the particular assignment. For example, the following could be a performance criteria list for a book report:

Criterion	Points
Cover illustration	10
Introductory paragraph presenting main theme	10
Four events presented in sequence in four paragraphs	20
Each body paragraph has a topic sentence	20
Each paragraph has three supporting detail sentences	15
Concluding paragraph restates main theme	10
Neatness and creativity	15
Total	100

◆ *Rubrics.* A rubric is a matrix that describes categories of performance, levels of mastery, and criteria for achieving each level of mastery. One example of a rubric for a persuasive essay is included in Figure 5.1. Students who are provided with rubrics before they begin an assignment have clear goals and well-defined expectations to guide their writing. Several Web sites provide teachers with sample rubrics that can be modified to meet specific goals (e.g., http://rubistar.4teachers.org or http://www.rubrics.com).

◆ *Focused Correction Areas.* Collins (1992) developed an instructional writing program for use across ages and curriculum areas

Category	Score				
	5	**4**	**3**	**2**	**1**
Format/ Process Pieces	Correctly formatted and has all required process pieces	One problem with formatting or one process piece missing	Two problems	Three problems	Four or more problems
Thesis	Thesis is last sentence of first paragraph and has subject details and purpose; is restated in first sentence of conclusion	Thesis is last sentence of first paragraph and is restated in first sentence of conclusion; either subject, details, or purpose unclear	Thesis incorrectly placed in first or last paragraph	Thesis is unclear or confusing, or is missing in first or last paragraph	Unidentifiable thesis
Mechanics	100% accurate; clearly proofread and edited; essay has good flow	1–2 minor errors that do not disrupt the flow	Several errors that prevent flow; careless spelling and typos	Many errors that distract the reader; grammar and spelling need attention	Major errors prevent the reader from understanding the topic
Content (Intro, Personal Background, During War, Lasting Influence, Conclusion)	Essay is within all minimum/ maximum paragraph limits	Essay has incorrect number of paragraphs in one area	Essay has incorrect number of paragraphs in two areas	Essay has incorrect number of paragraphs in three areas	Essay has incorrect number of paragraphs in four areas
Depth of Research	Essay is thorough, detailed, and leaves the reader without questions	Essay is generally thorough, but leaves a few loose ends	Essay shows some "holes" in research	Essay shows lack of understanding, leaves questions, or has errors in fact	Essay has major errors and/ or major gaps
Flow	Essay reads well, has good transitions	Essay generally has good flow; transitions need work	Essay is choppy; transitions are lacking	Essay is hard to follow in places, disorganized	Essay does not make sense in places; sentence or paragraph structure needs work

FIGURE 5.1. Example of a rubric for a persuasive essay. *Note.* Developed by Jamie D. Lyons, Diamond Middle School, Lexington, MA. Reprinted with permission.

that provides a structured teaching approach for five types of writing, from an informal brainstorm to a publishable work. The Focused Correction Areas (FCAs), used in the more complex writing assignments, provide criteria for evaluating the piece of writing. Focused correcting enables both students and teachers to address a few specific writing skills. Collins suggests that three FCAs be included for each assignment and that FCAs be mixed to include style, content, and organization (see Figure 5.2). The following is an example of three FCAs for an elementary assignment:

1. Three vivid verbs underlined
2. Topic sentences in each paragraph
3. Each sentence begins with a different word (sentence variety)

➡ ***Individualize goals for different students.*** In each classroom, students are at different stages in the development of their writing. Goals for writing can be individualized to match students' learning styles and levels of achievement. For example, remember Sara, Bill, and Tom from the reading lesson in Chapter 4 (see Table 4.2)? Table 5.2 describes the writing skills of these three students, now in middle school.

The following FCAs for these three students could challenge them by small degrees toward improvement based on their diverse learning profiles.

Sara

1. Each sentence begins with a different word
2. Graphic organizer completed and attached
3. Three adjectives underlined in each paragraph

Bill

1. All one-syllable words spelled correctly
2. At least five sentences in each paragraph
3. Graphic organizer completed and attached

Tom

1. Graphic organizer completed and attached
2. Clear topic sentence in each paragraph
3. Checklist of common errors attached

Directly Teach Prewriting Strategies

Students benefit from direct teaching of strategies for each stage of the prewriting process, from securing ideas to organizing ideas.

Examples of Focus Correction Areas for Style in Expository Writing

- No cliches or overused words
- No unnecessary words
- Word choice appropriate to purpose/audience
- No groups of short, monotonous sentences
- No long, confusing sentences
- Mix of sentence lengths and types (compound, complex, etc.)
- Powerful verbs
- Passive voice avoided

Examples of Focus Correction Areas for Content and Critical Thinking in Expository Writing

- Accurate, factual statement(s)
- Technical vocabulary used/spelled correctly
- Clearly stated thesis
- Sufficient facts and/or relevant details to support thesis
- Comparisons and contrasts
- Topic developed through facts and personal experience
- Examples used to support opinion
- References are current or reflect major resources

Examples of Focus Correction Areas for Organization in Expository Writing

- Introduction tells reader what writer intends to do and how it will be done
- Introduction draws reader into the work
- Conclusion reinforces thesis
- Conclusion sums up paper, brings to logical end
- Distinction between central and supporting ideas
- Transitions help reader move from point to point
- Paragraphs are coherent—have sense of purpose
- All unrelated ideas have been edited out

FIGURE 5.2. Examples of Focus Correction Areas for expository writing. *Note.* From *Developing Writing and Thinking Skills Across the Curriculum: A Practical Program for Schools* (pp. 18–19), by J. Collins, 1992, West Newbury, MA: Collins Education Associates. Reprinted with permission.

Secure ideas. At the beginning of the writing process, students search their brains for as many ideas as possible. The strategies used depend on the student's learning style and on whether the assignment is open-ended or structured by the teacher.

◆ *Brainstorming.* Individualized brainstorming procedures can accommodate students' learning styles. Students who demonstrate conceptual strengths can use a top–down procedure, whereby they first identify main ideas and themes and then generate relevant, supporting details. Students who overfocus on details at the

TABLE 5.2

Learning and Writing Profiles of Three Students

Sara	Bill	Tom
LD; processing skills are strong in the visual channel, weak in language; uses concrete language and sentences when writing	LD; strong oral language, good comprehension, poor phonological awareness; good ideas for writing but poor fluency, poor spelling and handwriting, limited production	ADHD; overfocuses on details, disorganized, poor self-monitoring

© 2006 by PRO-ED, Inc.

expense of the "big picture" can use a bottom–up procedure, whereby they first brainstorm critical vocabulary and details, then prioritize, and finally organize these details. (See examples of both procedures in Figure 5.3.)

◆ *Free writing.* During free writing, students write anything that comes to mind as fast as they can. They let their ideas flow without passing judgment on them. They then decide if any of these ideas has led them in a direction they wish to pursue further. For students who have difficulty with writing fluency, this activity can be made more gamelike through use of a "composition derby." The students and teacher free-write for a designated amount of time (2 to 5 minutes) and do not stop writing until time is called. Each student adds up the number of words written, and a total class score is computed and graphed for that day. (Alternatively, two teams can be formed and team points totaled.) Over time, class output should increase as fluency improves. Students can keep individual graphs and retain compositions for further development of ideas. This activity is particularly helpful for students with learning disabilities who often have difficulty with writing fluency (Rhodes & Dudley-Marling, 1988). Topics to stimulate free writing can be found in Appendix A.6, Mining for Topics.

◆ *Locating source materials for written papers.* Teach students how to locate sources for their paper, and how to choose appropriate active reading and note-taking strategies. Help students to find the system that works best for them. Demonstrate how to color-code note cards to correspond with specific sources. Research has indicated that, despite the emphasis on note-taking and outlining skills, few student writers make use of those techniques (Hillocks, 1986). (For additional note-taking strategies, refer to Chapter 7.)

➡ *Organize ideas.* This stage of the writing process is often the most difficult one for students who struggle with learning, attention, and

Top–Down Writing Sample

If I were a shoe what would my life be like?

Description	Experiences
smelling	stepped on
hot, sweaty	going everywhere
dirty	trips
white	vacations
~~black~~ brown	around town, malls
big, small	School (etc.)

feelings	Getting worn out
uncomfortable	getting dirty
hot	getting holes
grose	thrown away
broken in	worn everywhere
comfortable	years of use.

If I were a shoe, I would look much different than I ~~a~~ do as a person. as a new shoe I would be very white with other very distinct colors, but as I got ~~dirty~~ older and I was worn out and sweaty my color probably would change to brown dirt. also as I got older I would not be as ~~[illegible]~~ stiff and clean. along with my color changing ~~a~~ I would start to smell ~~[illegible]~~ and get very hot and sticky. But the dirtier and smellier I got, the more broken in and comfortable I would be.

Bottom–Up Writing Sample

Shoe
1 getting dirty
2 stepped on
3 smelly
5 hot, sweaty
worn out
1 getting holes
4 uncomfortable
2 traveling everywhere
4 attacked to a foot
1 thrown away

D ① Getting worn out
B ② experiences
A ③ description
C ④ feelings

If I were a ~~hot~~ sweaty and smelly shoe, life would be much different. as a shoe, I would go many places, and experience many new things. as time went by as an object stuck to a person's foot I would get stepped on and step on many things myself. as I grew older I would have ~~been~~ so worn out and so dirty from traveling and experiencing new things I would eventually be thrown away after many years of use.

FIGURE 5.3. Examples of top–down and bottom–up prewriting.

organization. However, this crucial step often makes the difference between a final product that is haphazard and difficult to follow, and one that is clear, fully elaborated, and easy to understand. Different planning and organizing strategies support various learning styles, and distinct strategies are appropriate for different types of writing.

➔ *Fiction*

Teachers need to help students understand the common elements that are present in most fictional stories, and then to use knowledge of the common literary structures to create their own fictional pieces.

◆ *Story maps.* A student's ability to write stories is dependent on his or her deep understanding of story structure (see Chapter 4). As an organizing strategy for writing, students complete a story map, or an outline, including the following basic elements (see example in Figure 4.2):

Setting: Time and place

Characters: Main characters, including physical and personal descriptions

Conflict: The problem in the story (three common conflicts, explained at the middle school level, are "person–person," "person–self," "person–society")

Plot: The events in the story

Resolution: How the problem is resolved

For students with learning difficulties, the Project Read Story Form provides instruction in understanding the "skeleton" of a story and the way in which each element fits into fictional stories (Greene & Enfield, 1999).

◆ *Story Grammar Marker.* For students who are kinesthetic learners, a hands-on version of a story map, called a Story Grammar Marker, has been created by Moreau and Fidrych-Puzzo (2002). The Story Grammar Marker includes all of the story elements, which are buttons or markers, spread out over a piece of yarn. The student can invent each element for writing as he or she holds each marker.

◆ *Star strategy.* The Star strategy (see Appendix B.2) can be used by writers of both fiction and nonfiction. The student places the main idea or title of the story in the center, and briefly answers the six questions placed in the points of the star (who, what, when, why, where, and how). The Star strategy is very flexible, and can be used across the curriculum and across grade levels (e.g., for a second-grade book report, a fifth-grade history paper, or a summary of a section of a middle school science textbook).

➔ *Nonfiction Reporting*

◆ *Understanding text structure.* Many students who have learning problems have particular difficulty organizing information and separating main ideas from relevant details in text. Similarly, when they begin to write reports, they may need assistance to focus on main themes and then to elaborate using relevant facts. Organizational strategies for nonfiction writing include linear models (outlining, lists) and graphic organizers (maps, webs).

◆ *Outlining.* The organizing strategies that enable students to understand text can help them create their own text. The outlining format described in the Project Read Report Form (Greene & Enfield, 1999) provides students with a structure for listing their title, subject, key ideas for each paragraph, and supporting details. The graphic organizer can be designed to be comprehensive or simple, depending on the students' age and ability. This type of outlining can be beneficial for both verbal and visual learners. Students with strengths in language and weaknesses in visual–spatial skills may benefit from learning systematic outlining procedures or using index cards to organize their ideas. When introducing a new organizational system for writing or note taking, provide a partially completed outline that allows students to fill in missing information. Decrease prompts for students as they gain proficiency.

◆ *Semantic mapping.* Once students have an understanding of basic text structures, students with strong visual–spatial skills can choose appropriate semantic maps to organize their writing (see Chapter 4). Using the brainstorming list, students group concepts together on the appropriate map. Figure 5.4 shows two examples from middle school students.

◆ *BOTEC.* BOTEC is an acronym and a visual image (robot) that is introduced in Essay Express, a CD-ROM designed to help students to write efficiently and easily (ResearchILD and FableVision, 2005). BOTEC can help upper elementary and middle school students organize their nonfiction writing. BOTEC is an acronym for remembering five steps in preparing to answer essay questions:

> **B**rainstorm
> **O**rganize
> **T**opic sentence
> **E**vidence
> **C**onclusion

◆ *Pieces of a Thesis.* To help students understand the components of an effective essay, it helps to create a real-life analogy. Because most students are familiar with the courtroom situation, this is an ideal analogy for persuasive essay writing.

- A lawyer needs to *prove* his or her case, as a writer needs to *prove* his or her thesis.
- A lawyer needs specific *evidence* to support his or her argument; a writer needs specific *evidence* to support his or her thesis.

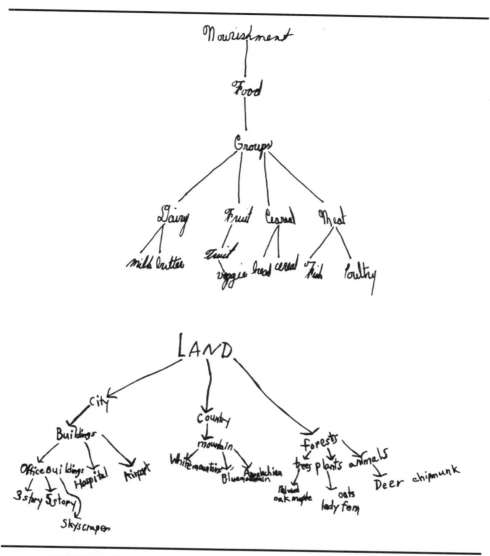

FIGURE 5.4. Two examples of semantic mapping.

- The lawyer must give an *opening statement* to the jury
  and end with a *concluding statement;* a writer begins
  with an introduction and ends with a conclusion.

This model, called Pieces of a Thesis, can be used for developing persuasive essays. A reproducible outline of the model is available in Appendix B.3.

Directly Teach Writing Strategies

Teach students to use self-regulation to guide their writing. During the composing process, students need to coordinate multiple sub-skills, processes, and strategies. Skilled writers use self-regulation to accomplish this purpose. Often, they talk to themselves while they write and give themselves verbal instructions as they go. Teachers can enhance students' use of self-talk by modeling their own self-instructions while writing. Harris and Graham (1992) described the following steps for teaching students how to use self-instructions in the context of strategy instruction.

1. When introducing a new strategy, the teacher first describes the strategy in detail. The teacher and students discuss why, how, and when to use it.

2. The teacher models the strategy while writing and uses appropriate self-talk during the process. These self-instructions can serve a number of purposes:
   - to identify problems as they are encountered (e.g., "What do I have to do here?")
   - to engage a particular strategy to solve the problem (e.g., "First, I will brainstorm ideas.")
   - to self-evaluate and self-correct when necessary (e.g., "Have I included all the parts to the story?")
   - to cope with frustrations (e.g., "I can handle this.")
   - to provide rewards (e.g., "I used great describing words.")

3. The teacher and students discuss the types of self-instructions used during the modeling.

4. Each student creates his or her own list of self-instructions, using teacher examples and the student's own ideas.

5. Students memorize examples from their personal self-instruction lists.

6. The teacher prompts students to use these self-instructions in various contexts until they become more automatic.

Students employ the target strategy and self-instructions as they write. The teacher offers support and assistance as needed. Over time, strategies are combined and self-regulation is expanded.

→ ***Work at the sentence level.*** Some students with learning problems need to use strategies designed to help them create sentences that are grammatically correct. As they become more adept as writers, they may benefit from strategies for elaboration, sentence variation, and vocabulary development.

◆ *Expanded kernel sentences.* This strategy, developed by Jennings and Haynes (2002), involves having students learn to write sentences in a specific sequence. Initially, they create simple noun–verb combinations, which they expand, first by adding "where" phrases, then "when" phrases, and then "where" and "when" phrases together.

◆ *The Project Read Framing Your Thoughts Curriculum.* The Project Read Framing Your Thoughts Curriculum expands the kernel sentence idea through use of multisensory strategies and symbols for each part of speech (Greene & Enfield, 1999). For students with significant learning issues, the Framing Your Thoughts Curriculum provides appropriate multisensory systematic instruction at the sentence level.

◆ *Elaboration.* Many beginning writers compose grammatically correct sentences that adequately describe main ideas. However, these students struggle to elaborate and describe their main points in a sufficiently sophisticated manner. Several strategies can help them.

1. *Adjective charts.* Charts of adjectives, grouped by type, can be helpful (Jennings & Haynes, 2002). For example, students can develop a general list of descriptive adjectives describing each of the five senses, color, number, and so on. They can refer to this chart whenever they are writing.

2. *Focused Correction Areas.* Many students need structured support to elaborate upon simple sentences. Collins's (1992) Focused Correction Areas, explained previously, provide one method for helping students to elaborate. Relevant FCAs may include (a) at least three adjectives in each paragraph; (b) at least six sentences in each paragraph; (c) at least five sensory details; and (d) one adjective for each of three senses: looks like, sounds like, feels like, and so on.

3. *Adjective awards.* Another idea is to assign points or "medals" based on the number of adjectives or adverbs used. For example, tell students that for a gold medal, they need 15 adjectives; for a silver medal, 10 adjectives; and for a bronze medal, 7 adjectives.

4. *Tell me more.* Pair each student with a peer. Each writes a topic sentence. Then one student asks the other to "tell me more" about the topic sentence. The partner talks through the details and then adds them to his or her written piece.

➡ ***Work at the paragraph level.*** Working at the paragraph level involves attention to sequences of sentences. Direct instruction in paragraph structure, as well as use of graphic organizers and key word lists, helps students with learning difficulties to write clearly.

◆ *Graphic organizers for paragraph development.* Many students have benefited from using the "Hamburger model" of a paragraph. The top bun represents the topic sentence; the hamburger, lettuce, tomato, and cheese represent supporting details; and the bottom bun represents the clincher, or concluding sentence. The students write their sentences in the appropriate boxes, and then copy them into a paragraph on a separate sheet of paper.

◆ *Using technology.* Students can practice organization of their writing by composing their paragraphs on the computer and then cutting apart the sentences and shifting them around to try out different ways of organizing their paragraphs.

◆ *Key word and transition word strategies.* After organizing their paragraphs using outlines or graphic organizers, students sometimes have difficulty formulating sentences. A simple strategy for sequencing sentences is to use the words *first, then, next, after that,* and *finally.* With these key words, students can summarize a story they read, create a story, describe a process, or correctly report events in their lives (Jennings & Haynes, 2002). As students become more adept as writers, they can substitute more complex transition words, which they can also use for multiparagraph essays (see Appendix B.4).

➜ **Work at the multiparagraph level.** Beginning in upper elementary and middle school grades, students need practice in combining paragraphs to make stories and essays. Students with learning difficulties benefit from explicit instruction, planning tools such as outlines and graphic organizers, and an essay construction process that builds essays one step at a time. The five-paragraph essay is an important form of essay construction. In the five-paragraph essay, the first paragraph is the introduction, the last paragraph is the conclusion, and the three middle or body paragraphs include the details or elaboration of the main ideas presented in the introduction and conclusion. A more sophisticated form of a five-paragraph essay is a persuasive essay written to prove a thesis.

◆ *Graphic organizers for essay development.* A good planning system for five-paragraph essays includes designing the blueprint in the same way an architect might design a house. Simple graphic organizers, with boxes for each paragraph, can help students with learning difficulties to outline their essays successfully (see Figure 5.5). Other students may benefit from using paragraph templates that include the leading few words from each paragraph to help students structure their writing (Jennings & Haynes, 2002; Tarricone, 1995).

Teach Self-Regulation Strategies

Teach Revision Strategies

➜ *Conferencing.* Conferences can be held regularly with a teacher or peer, or students can have "self-conferences" in which they ask themselves questions. These conferences provide verbal feedback about the students' writing and focus on the ideas rather than the

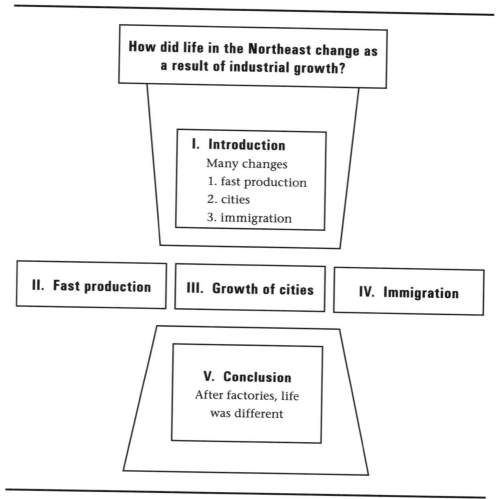

FIGURE 5.5. Example of a graphic organizer to plan a five-paragraph essay.

mechanics. Involving peers in conferencing activities helps students see the importance of writing for a variety of audiences. The feedback of fellow classmates encourages students to improve the clarity and level of detail in their writing. Students can read their writing aloud or have peers read it independently.

Three basic components can be included in each conference:

◆ *Tell back*. The teacher or peer summarizes the student's content to determine whether the reader's interpretation matches the writer's intended message.

◆ *Provide positive feedback*. The teacher reinforces appropriate use of strategies and skills. A peer discusses what he or she liked best about the writing. Writers with learning disabilities frequently exhibit negative attitudes toward their writing and lack confidence in their abilities. It is critical to provide positive feedback to these students about any skills and strategies used correctly or any improvements made, no matter how slight.

◆ *Provide constructive feedback.* The teacher introduces one or two new strategies or skills after discussing with the student which strategy or skill is needed to enhance the quality of the paper. For students with significant writing weaknesses, the teacher should focus on errors that occur frequently. The student records the new strategy or skill on a procedural checklist or into a strategy notebook. A peer provides feedback regarding what the writer needs to clarify in the writing.

The teacher keeps notes about the writing conference as part of the student's cumulative writing folder.

➡️ *Creating Sets of Criteria/Scales.* Students analyze model pieces of writing and develop sets of criteria that illustrate certain characteristics in the writing. Rating scales can be developed based on the criteria. Students apply these criteria to their writing and the writing of others. They identify ways to improve the writing and suggest revisions. Studies have indicated that use of structured criteria and scales was not only effective in improving students' revisions, but benefits were also noted on subsequent first drafts (Hillocks, 1986).

➡️ *Revision Techniques.* Students who do not have the benefit of word processors may be reluctant to revise if they dread having to rewrite. Various techniques, including the following, can be taught to students to simplify revisions:

• Write double-spaced drafts by skipping every other line to accommodate revisions.
• Cross out text that is being revised. Cross-outs are better than erasures, as the writer can still see the original text.
• Insert small pieces of new text using carets to indicate position.
• Insert larger pieces of new text with a numbering system or "spider legs" (e.g., strips of paper with the new text taped into the proper location).
• Reorganize using cut and paste.

Teach Self-Checking and Editing Strategies

➡️ *Editing Checklists.* Develop editing checklists with students based on their needs. Acronyms are often helpful.

◆ *COPS* reminds students to focus on **C**apitalization, **O**verall appearance, end **P**unctuation, and **S**pelling (Deshler & Schumaker, 1986). In the primary grades, COPS may be modified as **C**apitals, **O**rder, **P**eriods, and **S**pelling. In the middle grades, COPS can incorporate the skills needed from each student's perspective.

◆ An alternate acronym for the middle grades is STOPS (developed by Colin Meltzer, a sixth-grade student):

Sentence structure

Tenses

Organization/order

Punctuation

Spelling

This acronym is helpful for students who confuse verb forms and tenses.

◆ In high school, students can use SPORTS (developed by M. Perlmutter of ResearchILD):

Sentence structure

Punctuation

Organization

Repeated words

Tenses

Spelling

A picture of sports equipment may help trigger memory for the acronym in visual learners.

◆ For checking the answers to essays, especially those written in response to test questions, students can use QUEST, as in "Quest to do your best" (ResearchILD and FableVision, 2005). This checking strategy goes with the Pieces of a Thesis strategy (see Appendix B.3). Each letter represents a component to check in the essay.

- **Qu**estion: The student should consider, "Did I answer all the parts of the question? Did I answer the right question?"
- **E**vidence: The student should consider, "Did I include at least three details if possible, such as examples, dates, or names?"
- **S**ignal or transition words: The student should ask, "Did I use signal or transition words such as *also, however, another,* to connect ideas in my answer?"
- **T**opic sentences: The student should consider, "Does each paragraph have a good topic sentence? Did I start my essay with a topic sentence that introduces the main idea?"

Self-monitoring. Help students to develop awareness of their own errors. It is often challenging for students to find errors in their own writing. Sometimes, they read their writing the way they wanted it to sound, not the way they wrote it. Similarly, students are often inattentive to details. The following suggestions may help students identify their errors:

- *Changing to a different color pen for proofreading* helps students to change from the role of "writer" to that of "editor."
- *Reading their work aloud* helps students catch their errors.
- *Changing the background* of the word processor to black and the letters to white also helps students notice their errors.
- *Editorial assistance.* Students ask a teacher, parent, or peer editor to count the number of times a certain type of error occurred and to record this at the top of the page. Students then find their errors, counting to make sure they have found all of them.
- *Self-identification of errors.* Students circle words they know are misspelled, and underline words that might be misspelled. Students can mark suspected punctuation errors with a red pencil and then attempt correction.
- *Rewards for awareness.* To help students develop better self-monitoring skills, the teacher can reward *error identification* in the same manner as he or she rewards *correctness*.

Proofreading Paragraphs. Guide students through the proofreading process. Once students have found their common errors, the following strategies help them to correct these errors:

Problem:
Repetition of same word several times

Solution:
1. Use Franklin Wordmaster (electronic device); computerized thesaurus (keyboard shortcut Shift F7 in Microsoft Word); http://www.dictionaryreference.com on the Internet; or a traditional thesaurus to find synonyms.
2. Rearrange sentence to eliminate the repeated word.

Problem:
Inconsistent verb tense

Solution:
1. Decide on verb tense for writing (past, present, future).
2. Review writing and change tenses to stay consistent.

Problem:
Run-on sentences

Solution:
1. Break down wordy sentences (eliminate *and*).
2. Add signal words where appropriate (*however, first of all, finally, in other words,* etc.).
3. Use semicolons to break up sentences, if appropriate.

4. Remember the run-on rule: If you have to take a breath or two while reading the sentence aloud, it is a run-on.

Use Appropriate Technology

Using word processors allows students to focus on the ideas they are attempting to express. This reduces the demands on fine-motor skills, letter formation, and spatial organization that often impede the writing progress of students with learning difficulties. Students who use word processors may also be more apt to revise their writing, because they do not have to rewrite or "mess up" their papers. Students with learning difficulties need opportunities to revise easily in order to bypass their problems with handwriting and spelling; however, they also need opportunities to write with a pencil so they can practice and become more proficient.

Students with learning challenges may benefit from software designed specifically for writing. Examples include Write Outloud (Don Johnson), which reads back students' writing aloud and provides alternatives for spelling; Co-Writer (Don Johnson), a word prediction program that offers suggested words to complete phrases; and Dragon Naturally Speaking (Dragon Systems Software) or other speech-to-print software that can translate dictated speech into print. As with any strategy, each student responds differently to various technological solutions. For example, although speech-to-print software offers tremendous promise, the current state of the technology requires students to make many corrections in printed text. Correcting text may be so difficult or frustrating that the student finds the software unusable.

Link Assessment of Writing to Clear Expectations

Assessing student writing becomes easier when you begin with clear goal setting using performance-based criteria. Students can be graded based on their levels of achievement on the stated goals in their Focused Correction Areas or rubric. Giving students opportunities to improve their grades by revising their work enhances the learning process.

Sample Strategic Writing Assignment

How might you use these strategies during a writing lesson? Remember Sara, Bill, and Tom from the reading lesson discussed at the end of Chapter 4 (see Table 4.2)? Now imagine that it is 4 years later and they are in your eighth-grade English or social studies class. You have just completed a study of the Industrial Revolution in the United States, and you assign students in your class to write a five-paragraph essay. The class consists of 25 students in a heterogeneous grouping. Refer back to Table 5.2 for descriptions of the three students with learning disabilities and their writing skills.

Before Writing

→ *Establish purpose.* Discuss with students the purpose of the assignment: Students are expected to write a five-paragraph essay based on their study of the Industrial Revolution. Each student must describe how factories brought about changes in the northeastern United States in the 1800s. The purpose of the essay is to communicate their understanding of the topic and to integrate facts into a coherent essay. Devise a list of the specific Focused Correction Areas (FCAs; Collins, 1992) that students will be expected to master.

FCAs for the project
1. Introduction clearly states main idea (30 points)
2. Sufficient facts and/or relevant details to support main idea (40 points)
3. Three major industrial changes described (30 points)

→ *Determine accommodations.* For the three students with learning and attentional weaknesses in the class, modify FCAs as needed. For example, for Sarah, who is a strong visual learner, and Tom, who needs help with organization, use of a visual graphic organizer may be included in the FCAs and rewarded with points.

→ *Brainstorm.* Because this five-paragraph paper is historical in nature, ideas for the paper will come from the students' textbook and other source material available in class or through research. Students should gather their information and notes before beginning to write.

→ *Organize.* Students are often reluctant to take the time to use organizational strategies. They will be more likely to use them if the teacher requires them as part of the assignment. For this essay, students could use either a linear outline or a graphic organizer. An example of a graphic organizer was shown in Figure 5.5, and an example of an outline is shown in Figure 5.6.

During Writing

→ *Clarify expectations regarding writing skills.* Students should focus their first drafts on organization, creativity, and thematic continuity.

**Effects on Northeast of
Development of Factories**

I. **Introduction**
   A. Major changes in the Northeast occurred as a result of the events surrounding the development of factories.
   B. Three major changes:
      1. Goods produced faster
      2. Emergence of cities
      3. Immigration
II. **Change 1:** Faster production
   A. First, people spun by hand
   B. Next, water powered machines in mills
   C. Lots of yarn to trade
III. **Change 2:** Development of cities
   A. Factories near rivers
   B. People moved near factories
   C. Crowds
IV. **Change 3:** Immigration
   A. Search for work
   B. Different cultures and languages
V. **Conclusion:** Restate that life was different after factories.

FIGURE 5.6. Example of an outline for a five-paragraph essay.

Expectations for sentence structure, spelling, and mechanics are individualized based on students' abilities and editing checklists.

➔ *Establish timelines.* Provide calendars with due dates for various stages of the writing project. Develop study plans with students to help them achieve these goals. These plans can be individualized, and students with more significant organizational difficulties can be monitored more frequently than those who are well organized. Table 5.3 shows accommodations to address the individual learning styles of Sara, Bill, and Tom.

➔ *Model strategies to encourage self-regulation.* To model strategies for prioritizing information, complete with the class a graphic organizer that describes a topic in history that the students previously studied. For example, creating a graphic organizer describing events leading to the Revolutionary War would provide both spiral instruction in an earlier topic and a model for organization of the current topic. As

TABLE 5.3
Accommodations for Individual Learning Styles

Sara	Bill	Tom
Expected to use correct spelling and mechanics; sentence combining activities will be used to enhance grammatical complexity	Expected to use complex sentence structures with rich vocabulary and language usage; will use a word processor and spell-check feature, but drafts will not be checked for spelling; expected to use capitalization and ending punctuation only	Will develop a study plan with the teacher and set daily goals for the assignment and strategies for attaining these goals; will be responsible for all skills on his editing checklist

you create the organizer, talk through the process aloud, asking key questions and modeling self-regulation for the students.

After Writing

➡ *Revise for organization, creativity, and thematic continuity.*
- Help students revise their drafts and plan future directions through teacher and peer conferences. Students with difficulties in organization and prioritizing may need additional conference time. These can be scheduled into the projected timelines.
- Teach revision techniques.
- Students could use a word processor to minimize the fine-motor and organizational demands of writing.

➡ *Revise for sentence structure, spelling, and mechanics.*
- Teach students to combine brief sentences to help them develop more complex sentence structures.
- Teach students one or two more editing skills based on individual needs and include an editing checklist.
- Have students use their editing checklists to edit their papers.

Accommodations to help Sara, Bill, and Tom organize ideas are shown in Table 5.4. Accommodations for editing and revision for the three students are shown in Table 5.5.

TABLE 5.4

Accommodations To Help Students Organize Ideas

Sara	Bill	Tom
Use a *wh–* question list (i.e., *who, what, when, where, why, how*) to help her retrieve additional information to add to her concept map.	Have him draw lines on his map to assist his word alignment.	Structure this activity further by creating headings for each part of the map. This will help him to focus his ideas. Use *wh–* questions as with Sara.

© 2006 by PRO-ED, Inc.

TABLE 5.5

Accommodations To Help Students Revise and Edit

Sara	Bill	Tom
Have her circle frequently used words or concrete vocabulary and change these using a thesaurus.	Schedule additional conferences to help him revise for clarity and elaborate on his ideas (to increase productivity).	Schedule additional conferences to assist his development of topic sentences and his transitions between paragraphs.

© 2006 by PRO-ED, Inc.

Conclusion

Students with different learning profiles can be taught to write effectively if they are provided with strategies for writing that match their learning styles. Specific, concrete writing goals for each assignment, coupled with templates for organization, can assist students to meet grade-level criteria for well-developed writing skills. Conferences with teachers and careful editing of multiple drafts can provide the practice necessary for writers to become proficient.

Chapter 6

Math Strategy Instruction
Assessment for Strategic Teaching

*Before learning the strategies needed to become a successful math student,
the equations and formulas were scattered in my head and did not have
a place to go. Luckily, after learning to use three-column notes and other
techniques, I was able to sort them into little "file cabinets" in my head.*
                                                                    —Emily, 9th grader

Why Assess and Teach Strategies in Mathematics?

- In the past, there was an emphasis on either rote computation or meaningful problem solving. Currently, math students are required to become reasonably computationally fluent and to learn multiple strategies for solving math problems. Also, an increased emphasis has been placed in math classrooms on language, organization, and speed.
- The math curriculum in the early grades (Kindergarten to Grade 2) begins to focus on multiple learning strands (e.g., numbers and operations, algebra, geometry, measurement, and data analysis and probability).
- Learning mathematics and "showing what you know" now require skills in the process areas of problem solving, reasoning and proof, communication, connections, and representation (National Council of Teachers of Mathematics, 2000).

Students in math classrooms have diverse learning profiles. Some students are skillful math problem solvers who possess a subset of skills such as automatic recall of math facts, procedures, and problem-solving strategies; receptive and expressive language; visual–spatial perception and organization; sequencing; attention; working memory; and number sense. Students with math learning problems, however, who have a great deal of difficulty in one or more of these areas, struggle to learn basic math skills. For these students, direct systematic multisensory math instruction as opposed to a constructivist approach should supplement strategy instruction to reduce the incidence and severity of math-related learning problems. Assessment is a critical link to strategic math teaching.

All students can benefit from math strategy instruction. In particular, those students who have difficulty learning math in the classroom because of weaknesses in one or more of the following areas need strategic math instruction to compensate for their difficulties and to capitalize on their relative strengths.

What Cognitive and Linguistic Factors Underlie Students' Ability To Learn Math?	▥ Automaticity ▥ Sequencing ▥ Memory ▥ Visual–spatial organization ▥ Shifting mental sets easily and effectively (cognitive flexibility) ▥ Attention ▥ Planning and organizing ▥ Processing speed ▥ Receptive language ▥ Expressive language ▥ Emotional factors (i.e., motivation, anxiety, learned helplessness)

© 2006 by PRO-ED, Inc.

How Do Cognitive and Language Skills Affect Math Learning?

Although it is important to identify your students' prior math knowledge, it is also critical to be aware of any cognitive and linguistic skills that affect math learning in your class. You can gather this information by reading the neuropsychological and team evaluation reports in your students' files or by observing your students while they are working independently, in small groups, and with the entire class.

 Determine cognitive processes that may interfere with math performance. Consider whether your students
- have difficulty recalling facts due to problems with automatic memory;

- have difficulty with visual–spatial organization that affects their ability to align numbers or to understand concepts of quantity;
- understand the concepts, but have difficulty showing what they know due to difficulties with written output;
- appear to learn a concept one day, but then forget it soon after;
- have difficulty finishing their work;
- understand the concept but make "attentional" errors (e.g., add rather than subtract, misalign numbers, "forget" to reduce fractions); and
- answer impulsively.

Many students with learning problems, especially those who also have attention problems, often use random and impulsive approaches when solving math problems. When presented with a word problem, for example, they quickly call out, "I have to add, … no, multiply … no, subtract … divide?" These students benefit from learning organizational strategies that help them think through the problem, plan, and predict before they attempt to calculate and solve. Specific strategies (e.g., how to develop and use advanced graphic organizers) are described later in this chapter. These strategies also help students who cannot differentiate important and irrelevant information. You can encourage your students to think flexibly by helping them identify different ways to solve the same problem. Students can also learn how to use different strategies for various types of problems. For those students who have difficulty seeing part–whole relationships and analyzing patterns, you can demonstrate how particular patterns develop (e.g., Terrific Tens, discussed later in this chapter) so that they can begin to identify these patterns on their own.

 Determine language processes that may interfere with math performance. Consider whether your students
- understand verbal directions
- need you to reword your explanations
- need more "thinking time" before responding
- confuse the meaning of word problems
- have difficulty understanding math vocabulary (e.g., *times, divide, estimate, less than, all together*)

How Can You Forge a Link Between Assessment and Teaching in the Area of Mathematics?

In contrast to standardized tests that compare a student's performance with that of his or her peers, Assessment for Teaching has another purpose: to determine not only what a student has learned, but *how* he or she learns, with the purpose of informing future instruction (Meltzer, 1993a, 1993b; Roditi, 1993).

→ ***Consider psychoeducational diagnostic assessment with a mathematics component.*** The difference between a mathematics evaluation and a psychoeducational evaluation is that math tests identify *what* your students do and do not know in various strands of the mathematics curriculum, whereas a psychoeducational assessment describes *how* your students learn and perform on math tasks. Math assessment frequently confirms what you already know about your students from observing them in class. The results often pinpoint specific gaps in your students' knowledge of quantitative concepts and skills (i.e., addition/subtraction, multiplication/division, fractions, decimals, percentages, time, measurement, and geometry). Typically, the results are based on the accuracy of your students' answers and yield a grade-score equivalent. Traditional, subject-centered forms of math assessment are effective in identifying what math skills to teach. From results of psychoeducational evaluations, however, you become aware of your students' cognitive and learning profiles. By matching students' learning styles with specific strategies and teaching methods, you give students opportunities to succeed in math. You build their self-confidence so they perceive themselves as capable math problem solvers for the first time. You can use a learning profile Venn diagram (see Appendix B.5) to help summarize each student's strengths and weaknesses.

→ ***Consider using the principles of diagnostic math educational therapy (MET).*** Standardized tests can be excellent tools to identify gaps in your students' math knowledge base. Some of your students may already have been tested and you know that they need to improve certain skills. However, you still do not know how to teach them so that they can learn and succeed. MET, an Assessment for Teaching technique, provides information about *what* a student knows and *how* a student learns and performs best. In approximately eight 45-minute sessions of working one-to-one with a student, a teacher can identify areas of strength and can notice where the breakdown occurs in the process of learning math. Although many teachers may not have the opportunity to work one-to-one with a student for eight sessions, MET principles can be adapted and used in classrooms, resource rooms, and clinical settings. A sample MET report can be found in Appendix A.7.

→ ***Use an organizational framework to ensure that you are covering the critical processes of math assessment and instruction.*** One example of an organizational framework follows:

A CLAP

Automaticity—automatic memory for math facts

Concepts—understanding the quantitative concept through concrete, semiconcrete or representational, and abstract levels

Language—the language of math (vocabulary, language of instruction, translating "English" to math)

Applications—the way the concepts and procedures are used in the real world (i.e., problem solving)

Procedures—the systematic way to solve math problems (e.g., algorithms, "road maps" for solving word problems, procedures for using a calculator)

→ *Evaluate your students' understanding of quantitative concepts and symbols.* Assess students' number sense, or the ability to understand quantitative concepts and the meaning of numbers. Students with math learning problems often exhibit cognitive strategy deficits that manifest in the lack of an intuitive number sense. Math assessment should help you differentiate students who do and do not have a strong number sense and determine under what conditions numbers become meaningful. Below are some principles to guide your assessment for teaching number sense.

◆ Observe your students while they engage in various math activities to see if they are attaching meaning to numbers. For example, in the primary grades, are they counting, using one-to-one correspondence, or determining which group or which student has more of something?

◆ Use multisensory formats for assessment and teaching.

◆ Use dialogue to check your students' understanding of quantitative concepts and symbols.

◆ Determine whether your students are at the number, algorithm, or application level of number sense:

Number Level
- Digit meaning (*7*)
- Number word meaning (*seven*)
- Number word meaning in real-life context (*seven cars*)

Algorithm Level
- Operation symbol meaning
- Rules or procedures (i.e., long division using only numbers without context)
- Rules or procedures in the context of a meaningful problem

Application Level (i.e., problem solving)
- Effective selection and use of cognitive strategies
- Checking reasonableness of partial and final solutions

At the number level, some students look at the digit symbol 7 and automatically attach meaning to it, whereas other students look at the same digit 7 and think they are reading a foreign language. At the *algorithm* level, students are expected to associate quantitative concepts with specific operational symbols (e.g., + means addition). At the *application* level, students must rely on their number sense to make sure the problem-solving process and solution make sense.

◆ Continually question *how* you can make meaningful mathematical connections for students who have compromised number sense by asking questions such as the following:

- Have I paired number symbols with graphic representations?
- Does the use of concrete aids enhance number meaning or hinder it for a particular child?
- Should I pair concrete aids with verbal discussion and make connections to real-life experience?
- Should all numbers be presented in a real-life context?

Strategic Math Teaching

Once you understand your students' strengths and weaknesses, select strategies that will enhance your students' ability to learn the new material you plan to introduce into your math class. Here are some examples of questions to guide your math strategy instruction:

- Which students need to learn which strategies?
- Which students will benefit from practicing a draw-it-out strategy, where they create a picture or diagram to help them understand the mathematical information, as opposed to an organized list strategy, where they list the information in chart form?
- Which students will need more time to practice their multiplication facts?
- Which students will benefit from enrichment projects or curriculum extensions?
- How can you create various flexible groupings to focus on the various strategies that different learners need to learn or practice?
- Have you paired number symbols with graphic representations?
- Does the use of concrete aids enhance number meaning or hinder it for a particular child?
- Should concrete aids be paired with verbal discussion and connections made to real-life experience?
- Should all numbers be presented in a real-life context?

You can be strategic—that is, you can decide what teaching methods and materials to use and how to use them most effectively in a classroom where students have multiple learning profiles.

Helping Students To Build Automaticity: Math Facts, Rules, and Vocabulary

Teaching Math Fact Recall

Timed tests on math facts and complex computations pose problems for many students with learning difficulties. They often show weaknesses in their automatic memory for math facts, resulting in slow, effortful, and often inaccurate calculations. By identifying these students early, you can provide them with direct strategic math instruction to tackle this particular problem. By doing so, you can prevent them from experiencing years of frustration and failure in math.

Until recently, you most likely relied on drill-and-practice activities using flash cards, fact table exercises, and worksheets to help your students memorize the basic math facts. Many students with learning difficulties, however, need even more systematic, strategic approaches to build speed and accuracy for recalling math facts. New research-based techniques and computer technology offer teaching methods that do help students who have found it next to impossible to automatize their math facts. Hasselbring, Goin, and Bransford (1988) provided a systematic, research-based technique for helping students with learning difficulties learn how to automatize math facts. Here are some important principles and guidelines to follow:

- Assess students' current level of math fact recall.
- Use direct, systematic, multisensory approaches.
- Build on your students' prior knowledge to select new facts to learn.
- Focus strategy instruction on only two or three related math facts at a time.
- Teach number families.
- Create card games.
- Teach strategies for accuracy before building speed.

→ *Assess current level of automaticity (**math fact recall**).* From observations of students' work in math class, you may be able to identify some, but not all, students who have or have not automatized their math facts. Some students develop their own idiosyncratic strategies for figuring out math facts that they have not automatized, but this extra mental work soon becomes inefficient. As problem-solving demands increase, these students can no longer divert their attention to figure out a fact and refocus their attention on the problem at hand. Math assessment can identify those students who compensate for a lack of automaticity and can pinpoint those specific math facts that are problematic. It is important to note that the math facts that should be automatized are addition and multiplication facts. The other facts (subtraction and division) can be learned through number families and analogous facts so that students can be reasonably fluent with computation.

→ *Use a direct, systematic, multisensory approach with strategy instruction.* By using a systematic approach to assess the automatic recall of math facts, you can differentiate math facts into three distinct groups:

Three Kinds of Math Facts	▥ *Autofacts*—Math facts your student has automatized ▥ *Stratofacts*—Math facts your student can figure out slowly using an idiosyncratic strategy (strategically computed) ▥ *"Clueless" Facts*—Math facts your student cannot recall at all (completely unknown)

Math fact grids, either teacher-made or purchased, are excellent visual aids for documentation (see example in Figure 6.1). By analyzing automatic memory of facts, you help your students realize that memorizing math facts can be simplified. When the number of facts to learn is reduced, the task becomes less overwhelming and less of a working memory load. This grid can be used as part of the teaching process, to chart the students' progress. This is a valuable tool for students, as they can see their growth in a concrete, visual way.

→ *Build on students' prior knowledge.* Determine whether your students demonstrate knowledge of the following rules and strategies, and then teach them how to build on their current knowledge.

→ *Addition*
◆ *One-up (+1) Rule (up-one rule, add-on-one rule, or incrementing rule).* Many students enjoy "naming" the rule themselves. Active involvement often increases their chances of remembering and applying the rule later. Most elementary students can easily apply this rule. They soon realize that they now "own" 20 more

	0	1	2	3	4	5	6	7	8	9
0										
1										
2										
3										
4										
5										
6										
7										
8										
9										

A—Autofact   S—Stratofact   U—Unknown Fact

FIGURE 6.1. A math fact grid.

facts on the 100-space math fact grid, thus motivating them to automatize more facts.

Students who have learned that 1 + 1 = 2, 2 + 1 = 3, and so on, can be taught, for example, that 151 + 1 = 152. They also can be taught generalizations, such as 1 + 2 = 3 and 1 + 151 = 152.

◆ *Doubles rule.* Students tend to remember the doubles easily (e.g., 1 + 1 = 2, 2 + 2 = 4). They enjoy accumulating 10 more facts, thus adding to their repertoire of stratofacts.

◆ *+2 Strategies.* You can teach students two +2 strategies.

- *Use the one-up rule twice:* Some students quickly learn to use their prior knowledge of the +1 rule and use the rule twice in a row. They find an autofact, such as 6 + 0 = 6; then they can produce 6 + 1 = 7, then 6 + 2 = 8 by mentally incrementing twice.

• *Use a visual, counting-up approach:* Teach the students to count up twice from the larger number.

$0 + 5 = 5$
$5 + 0 = 5$
$5 + 1 = $ ▢▢▢▢▢ $+$ ▢ $= 6$
$5 + 2 = $ ▢▢▢▢▢ $+$ ▢▢ $= 7$

◆ *Teach the "TEEN" strategy.* By using both the sound of your voice to emphasize "teen" and the capitalized printed syllable TEEN, you can help those students who need visual and/or auditory cues to remember the TEEN facts:

$10 + 3 = $ thir TEEN $= 13$	$3 + 10 = $ thir TEEN $= 13$
$10 + 4 = $ four TEEN $= 14$	$4 + 10 = $ four TEEN $= 14$

◆ *Teach the "Terrific Tens" strategy directly.* Some students with learning difficulties do not recognize patterns until you develop a pattern with them. The pattern in Figure 6.2 for adding two numbers to equal 10 helps students see that as they increase one number across the top, they decrease a number across the bottom. They can visualize the generalizations. Those students who cannot easily remember the math facts by rote quickly learn that they can generate 10 facts from one fact. If they know that $1 + 9 = 10$, they can figure out the rest of the pattern themselves (see also Figure 6.3, which shows the same strategy using cards).

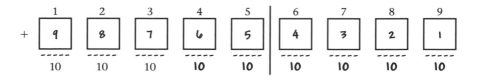

FIGURE 6.2. The "Terrific Tens" strategy.

FIGURE 6.3. Example of "Terrific Tens" strategy for memorization of math facts.

→ *Multiplication*

◆ *Identify a pattern of strategies that emerges and create a checklist with your students to figure out difficult facts.*

- 0 rule (0 times any number is 0)
- 1 rule (1 times any number is the number itself)
- 2s rule (Counting by 2s [even numbers] for 2 times table)
- Does the number end in a 5 or a 10? (Counting by 5s or 10s)
- 9s rule
- Count backwards (for 8 × 7)
- Count backwards by 2s (e.g., 6 × 4)

◆ *Teach the 9s rule.* Students are fascinated when they learn the "magical" 9s rule of multiplication. They can use their prior knowledge of all the numbers that add up to 9 (e.g., 4 + 5, 3 + 6, 2 + 7, and 1 + 8). They can also use a count-backwards strategy to find the first number. This strategy, together with students' prior knowledge of easier 9s facts, helps them recall the 9s facts quickly. An example is shown in Figure 6.4.

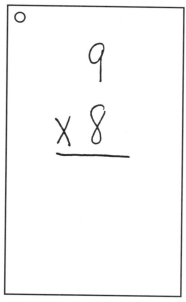 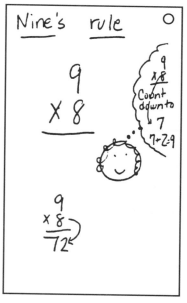

front   back

FIGURE 6.4. An example of use of the 9s rule.

◆ *Teach a count-backwards strategy for 8 × 7 = 56 (see Figure 6.5).*

◆ *Teach a count-backwards-by-2s strategy for 6 × 4 = 24 or 7 × 6 = 42 (see Figure 6.6).*

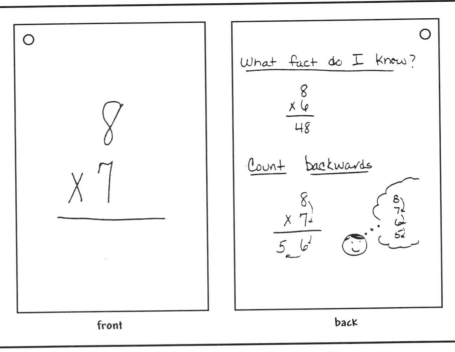

front   back

FIGURE 6.5. A count-backwards strategy for 8 × 7 = 56.

◆ *Teach strategies in combination with prior knowledge of a mastered fact.* For example, if your students know that 7 × 5 = 35, they know that the next group of 7s will be in the 40s (7 × 6 = __).

◆ *Build speed gradually.* As your students enter your classroom, give each a different math fact to recall (one of their new

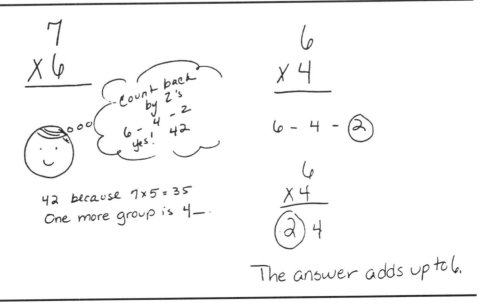

FIGURE 6.6. A count-backwards-by-2s strategy for 6 × 4 = 24 or 7 × 6 = 42.

facts). You can time them by holding your hand up high and gradually letting it fall as you count out seconds. You can snap your fingers at the 5-second count to see if your students can recall the fact that quickly. Then, you can reduce the number of seconds before you snap your fingers to show your students that they are recalling the facts more quickly. Their time may improve from 5 seconds to 1 second, and then they become automatic in their recall.

◆ *Teach mnemonic strategies.* For example, a verbal mnemonic could be a rhyme such as "6 and 7 didn't have a clue until they met 42." A visual mnemonic for the 3 times table consists of a stoplight: The "red facts," 3 × 1, 3 × 2, and 3 × 3, are the children under 10, who have to "stop" before they can do many activities independently; the "yellow facts," 3 × 4, 3 × 5, and 3 × 6, are the teens who need to use caution; and the "green facts," 3 × 7, 3 × 8, and 3 × 9, are all adults in their 20s. This strategy comes from *Math in Bloom* (Schroeder & Washington, 1989).

➡ ***Focus strategy instruction on only two or three related facts at a time.*** Encourage your students to develop strategies that capitalize on their strengths and interests. Students may benefit from collecting facts that they are learning on a "math ring," a collection of facts on index cards, held together by a notebook ring. The ring could emphasize mastered facts rather than "facts to learn" and strategies for remembering the correct answers. Collecting facts on a math ring can be very rewarding and can provide an incentive to add on more and more facts (see Figure 6.7). A fact is written on one side of a card, perhaps with a "strategy cue" in the corner. The answer and the strategy are written on the back. Students with learning difficulties

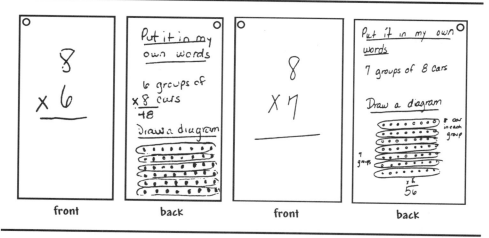

FIGURE 6.7. An example of cards on a math ring.

often require continual review of newly automatized facts to store these facts in their long-term memory. Students can place math rings in a convenient place as a reminder to review these on a daily basis. Some teachers ask their students to place their math rings inside their math strategy notebooks for use during practice lab or "strategy time." These practice labs are described in more detail later in this chapter.

Teach number families. Number families are clusters of related math facts, including addition and subtraction (or multiplication and division) and their related facts (see Figure 6.8). The following are problems in a number family:

$$1 + 9 = 10 \qquad 9 + 1 = 10 \qquad 10 - 1 = 9 \qquad 10 - 9 = 1$$

You can ask your students to represent these number sentences in various ways. Some students could draw objects representing these number sentences. Students who have difficulty drawing could use math manipulatives. You are helping all students to understand that addition and subtraction, or multiplication and division, are interrelated concepts, not discrete operations. Further, you are helping stu-

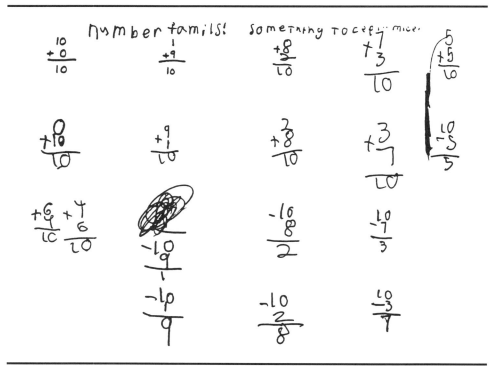

FIGURE 6.8. Number families: A strategy for learning clusters of related addition and subtraction facts.

dents with memory weaknesses. By clustering numbers in this way, your students only have to retrieve one family of math facts that unleashes the other facts rather than remembering many separate math facts. By using a multisensory approach during this process whereby the students "talk" and "hear" math facts, picture them, and write about them, you can rest assured that you are addressing the multiple learning styles in your classroom.

→ *Create card games.* Students with learning difficulties need more reinforcement and spiral teaching than the average student. Drill and practice can be effective if implemented within a card game context. The advantage of using cards is the pairing of the number symbols and graphic representations simultaneously, thereby enhancing number sense while building automaticity. Fraction cards are also available that pair the fraction with a visual drawing that represents the same fraction.

→ *Teach strategies for accuracy before building speed.*
- Teach mnemonic strategies for recall of math facts.
- Provide successful experiences by simplifying what is perceived by some students to be an overwhelming task.
- Present one rule that teaches approximately 20 facts (e.g., the 9s rule).
- Help your students create math rings to collect math strategies.
- Gradually build speed after strategies have been mastered.

Teaching Rules and Vocabulary

→ *"Talk" mathematics in a thoughtfully sequenced way.*
- Use dialogue that begins at a point of prior knowledge.
- Teach rules directly.
- Give many examples.
- Set up question–answer sequences so that they lead to successful responses.

→ *Summarize rules, formulas, and algorithms verbally and visually.*
- Remember to use a multisensory approach.
- Have your students repeat rules orally in their own words.
- Draw a rule box on the chalkboard (visual).
- Give students time to write in their math strategy notebooks.
- Model on the board or on the overhead how students can summarize rules. Teach students to make summary boxes or stategy clouds in their strategy notebooks (see Figure 6.9).

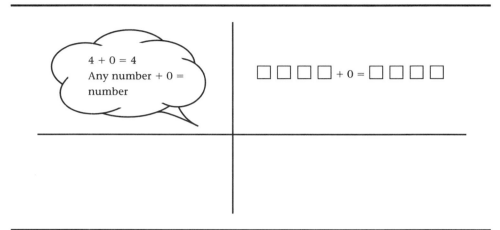

FIGURE 6.9. Strategy clouds or summary boxes for summarizing math rules.

➡ ***Teach three-column note-taking strategy to link symbolic representations of numbers with graphic representations*** (see Figure 6.10). You can teach your students, as early as first grade, how to take three-column notes by modeling the process with them using the overhead projector. An effective way to begin is to start with vocabulary words or the problem to solve in the first column, the definition of the word or the "golden rule" (the strategy to use to solve the problem, e.g., the 9s rule) in the second, and a picture or a visual example in the third column.

Problem or Vocabulary Word	Golden Rule or Strategy	Example

FIGURE 6.10. A sample three-column form to summarize math rules.

Additional Teaching Strategies

➡ ***Use software programs.*** To enhance automaticity further, you can provide your students with an opportunity to practice only the autofacts and two new stratofacts without confusing the situation with clueless facts. Some software programs allow you or your students to program only those math facts being practiced into the computer-based activity. The aim is to increase the repertoire of stratofacts gradually, to the point that timed practices may begin. Software programs that allow you to manage the level of difficulty include Number Maze Challenge (Great Wave Software) for untimed practice and Math Blaster (Knowledge Adventure) for timed practice.

➡ **Set up practice labs in your classroom (structured opportunities for guided practice).** Set aside time (5 to 15 minutes) during the day for all students to practice a particular skill or strategy. During these practice labs, you can individualize or group students so that they can work on their own instructional goals. By using math strategy notebooks and flexible groups, these practice labs can be effective for the slow learner, the gifted student who needs time for curriculum extension, those students who need more time to process information and to complete their work, and those students who simply need time to practice.

➡ **Decide when it is appropriate to encourage calculator use and when to avoid it.** The National Council of Teachers of Mathematics emphasizes that all students should be "reasonably fluent in computation," yet there remains a focus on conceptual understanding and problem solving as well. If the goal of your lesson is to teach students to be more automatic with math fact recall, using a calculator is not helpful. If, on the other hand, you are teaching an algorithm and want your students to see how number patterns develop, the calculator can be a useful teaching tool. Students who have difficulty automatically retrieving math facts and procedures need access to a calculator whenever they are introduced to new concepts and procedures, as well as when they are problem solving. This enables them to focus on solving the problem rather than remembering a random fact. If your curriculum continues to emphasize paper-and-pencil calculations, you can minimize the amount of teaching time spent on this soon-to-be-obsolete skill in our technological society. At least allow your students to check their answers with a calculator. Some students may prefer to use a calculator with a printout to check for accuracy. Others, who have memory and organizational difficulties, may need to write down each numerical entry before entering the numbers into the calculator.

Helping Students Learn To Problem Solve

Review the mathematical problem-solving process and analyze where your students may be encountering initial difficulty (see Table 6.1). Some students

TABLE 6.1

Mathematical Problem-Solving Process

Goals	Ask yourself: Can my student ...
Reading	read the problem independently?
Orientation	conceptualize the problem?
Transfer	translate the problem from one representation to another (shift sets among words, pictures, objects, tables, graphs)?
Organization	plan a path to the solution?
Calculation	calculate?
Verification	monitor the course of solution?

break down immediately because they cannot read the problem due to a read-ing disorder rather than a math disability. Many other students who can read and understand the problem experience significant difficulty at the transfer phase and the organization phase. Once you are aware of the breakdown, there are a number of strategies that you can teach your students to overcome this problem.

 Teach students using systematic, multisensory techniques. To make your teaching presentations accessible to all learners, concrete aids should be used as math lab materials from elementary school through college. Verbal explanation and classroom discourse must accompany the visual models and hands-on learning to help those students with visual–spatial difficulties to connect meaning with numbers. Miller and Mercer's (1993) CSA Multisensory Technique—**C**oncrete (use hands-on manipulatives), **S**emiconcrete (use and create pictures), and **A**bstract (pair numerical symbols with concrete and semicon-crete aids)—is one example of a research-based teaching method that embodies multisensory instruction in a structured and systematic way. Systematic multisensory instruction in mathematics also occurs in lessons based on Sharma's (1989) "Six Levels of Knowing." The important principle is that each lesson embodies systematic, multi-sensory instruction that is explicit and direct. Lessons include spiral teaching so that students have ample opportunities for review and making meaningful connections.

Some students cannot conceptualize quantitative concepts unless they are presented first in a concrete manner within a mean-ingful context. Some students who have language difficulties can benefit from pictures and hands-on manipulatives. Students who have visual–spatial difficulties often rely on verbal explanations and discussions that combine visual models with hands-on learning. In some manipulative programs, the numbers are not systematically paired with the concrete aids. Some students need the teacher to make those connections explicit.

➡ *Minimize the number of strategies your students need to learn.* Many students with math learning difficulties may be confused and disorganized when learning about the various problem-solving strategies they are supposed to learn. Figure 6.11 lists the problem-solving strategies (Coburn, Hoogeboom, & Goodnow, 1989) that are part of elementary and middle school math problem-solving curricula. Students with learning disabilities and attention-deficit/hyperactivity disorder (ADHD) need to be taught how to select an appropriate strategy and how to organize the information in a systematic way.

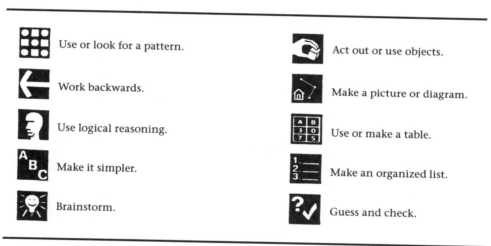

FIGURE 6.11. Problem-solving strategies for math curricula. From *The Problem Solver with Calculators,* by T. G. Coburn, S. Hoogeboom, and J. Goodnow, 1989, Mountain View, CA: Creative Publications. Copyright 1989 by Creative Publications. Reprinted with permission.

➡ *Use graphic organizers, and teach students how to create their own graphic organizers.* Some students can organize information from a word problem or a table without your help, but others need structure and visual support to organize all the relevant mathematical information they need to solve a problem. Graphic organizers, especially those students create themselves with your help, are effective tools for learning how to solve word problems systematically. The work sample shown in Figure 6.12 is an example of a list strategy used by a second-grade student who has a strength in this area. However, students who are inherently disorganized, especially students who have learning disabilities or ADHD, need to be taught how to organize relevant information.

calories: orange 65,
wheat bread 130,
egg 80,

onser: 275

Jed had an orange, 2 slices of wheat bread, and an egg for breakfast. How many calories were in Jed's breakfast?

Calories in Foods

Food	Calories
Wheat bread (1 slice)	65
Cereal (1 ounce)	110
Milk (1 cup)	124
Banana	100
Orange	65
Egg (medium)	80

FIGURE 6.12. Work sample of a second-grade student, Michelle, showing how the student organized information from a word problem. From *TOPS Calculator Problem Deck IV,* by C. Greenes, G. Immerzerl, L. Schulman, and R. Spungin, 1989, Palo Alto, CA: Dale Seymour Publications. Copyright 1989 by Dale Seymour Publications. Reprinted with permission.

Figure 6.13 is an example of a fourth-grade student's personally designed graphic organizer that was meaningful to him. The Ninja Math graphic reminded him to take the time to plan and to be systematic in his approach. After a while, he began to internalize and visualize his organizational strategy so that he no longer had to draw out the entire figure.

Figure 6.14 is another example of a student-created organizer that helped a student to solve word problems systematically. The student, Keith, created a strategy called RAPM:

Read & **R**ap (read the problem and repeat in own words)
Art (represent the problem by drawing a diagram)
Plan & **P**redict (think of a plan for solving the problem, and predict the answer)
Melvin the calculator (use a calculator; in this case the student named his calculator Melvin)

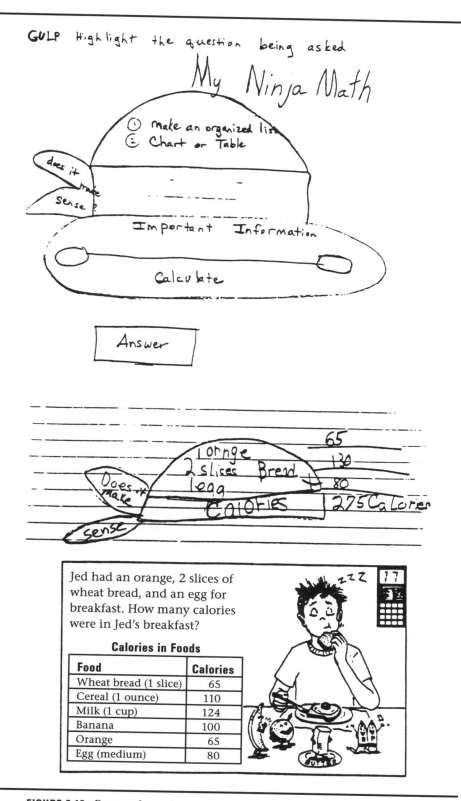

FIGURE 6.13. Personal graphic organizer developed by Colin, then a fourth-grade student.

A restaurant manager has 144 flowers. She wants to put the same number on each of 24 tables. How many flowers can she put on each table?

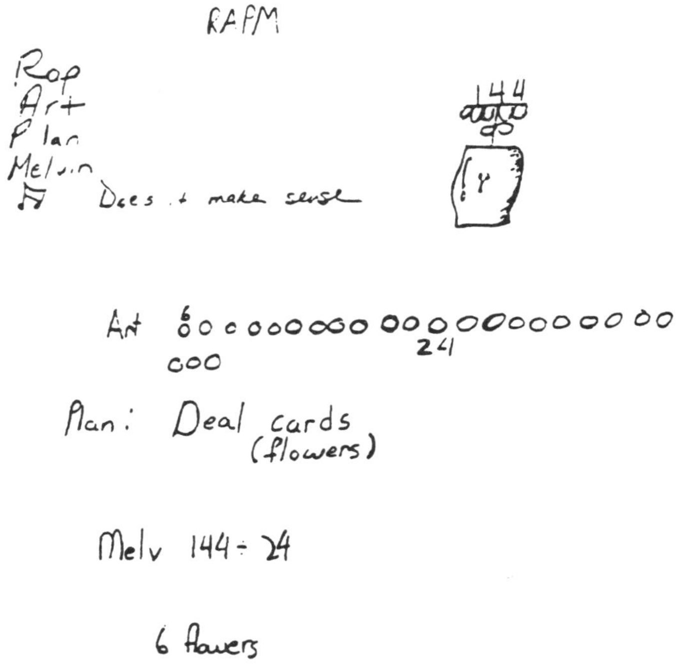

RAPM

Rap
Art
Plan
Melvin
M   Does it make sense

144
÷24

[?]

Art   6 o o o o o o oo oo oo ooooooo oo
o o o   24

Plan: Deal cards
(flowers)

Melv 144 ÷ 24

6 flowers

FIGURE 6.14. Another example of a student-created organizer to help solve word problems.

Then Keith sings to himself, asking the question, "Does it make sense?" Many students, like Keith, rely on writing RAPM each time they begin a new problem. Over time, students internalize the process and need to write out the steps only when they encounter a more difficult problem. For example, as shown in Figure 6.14, the RAPM strategy can be applied multiple times to help solve multiple-step problems.

➡ *Teach checking strategies directly.* Students often forget to check their work, and students with learning problems often do not know how to check their work systematically. You can assist by helping them to create their own personalized checklists of questions that tap typical errors. The first step is to do an error analysis. Using class-work or tests, help your students identify common errors. When the students are allowed to make corrections on tests, ask them, "How many questions were careless errors? How many errors were because you misread the directions?" Another approach is to ask a parent volunteer or the special education teacher to analyze three or four tests and identify the trend in error types. Once the error analysis is complete, you can identify the most common errors for a student or the class. The following is an example of a math checklist.

Example of a Math Checklist	▥ Did I write down the numbers correctly? ▥ Did I line up the numbers correctly? ▥ Did I confuse the direction of the *x* and *y* when I graphed? ▥ Is my answer close to my estimate? ▥ Did I make any sign errors? ▥ Did I add when I was supposed to multiply? ▥ Did I label my answer correctly ($, units)?

Many students will never remember such a long list. You can help them by prioritizing and identifying the three errors they most often make. Here is an example of a condensed math checklist:

Top Three Hits
1. Label the units
2. Any sign errors?
3. Does the answer make sense?

Some students may remember to check more consistently if they use an acronym. One such acronym is POUNCE. Visualize a cat, pouncing on the math problem or test to check it. This strategy enables the student to switch his or her mindset from that of a student to that of a teacher, in order to "catch" errors more reliably.

P—Change to a different color **pen** or **pencil** in order to change your mindset from that of student (test taker) to teacher (test checker).

O—Check **operations.**

U—**Underline** the question (in a word problem) or the directions. Did you answer the question? Did you follow directions?

N—Check the **numbers.** Did you copy them down correctly? In the right order?

C—Check your **calculations.** Check for the type of calculation errors you tend to make.

E—Does your answer agree with your **estimate?** Does your answer make sense?

➡ ***Teach strategies in algebra.*** At the middle and high school levels, all students, especially those with learning difficulties, benefit from a strategic way to remember the steps in algebraic procedures. Good examples are the FOIL and Face strategies used to factor polynomials. Typically, FOIL is taught as an acronym for multiplying the **F**irst terms, **O**utside terms, **I**nside terms, and **L**ast terms. Some students cannot remember the FOIL trick or they typically make sign errors when they are adding the middle terms. You can provide an alternative strategy, Face, for those students who need a more visual or meaningful strategy. Figure 6.15 demonstrates Face, which is an effective strategy to focus visually on the algebraic sign of the middle terms, a troublesome area for many students. Note that the three forms of factoring are summarized for the students in a list form that also utilizes visual cues. You can write this list on the overhead or on the board, and the students can copy it into their math strategy notebooks.

Factoring

1. Greatest Common Factor

2. $\square^2 - \square^2$
   Difference
      between
         Two Squares

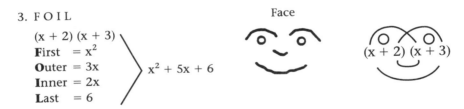

3. F O I L
   $(x + 2)\ (x + 3)$
   First $= x^2$
   Outer $= 3x$
   Inner $= 2x$ $x^2 + 5x + 6$
   Last $= 6$

Face

$(x + 2)\ (x + 3)$

FIGURE 6.15. Three forms of factoring. FACE is an effective strategy to prevent typical sign errors.

Teach strategies in geometry. In geometry, students often confuse the multiple attributes of various geometric shapes. By developing flow diagrams and lists with your students, you can help them to understand the interrelationships among the various geometric shapes. Some textbooks provide diagrams like the one in Figure 6.16; however, developing the diagram with your students as an organizing framework is more effective than simply giving them the diagram as another memorization task.

Figure 6.17 is another example of how a graphic organizer can be used. This time, a new concept and a set of part–whole relationships are developed using manipulatives (geoboard and elastics),

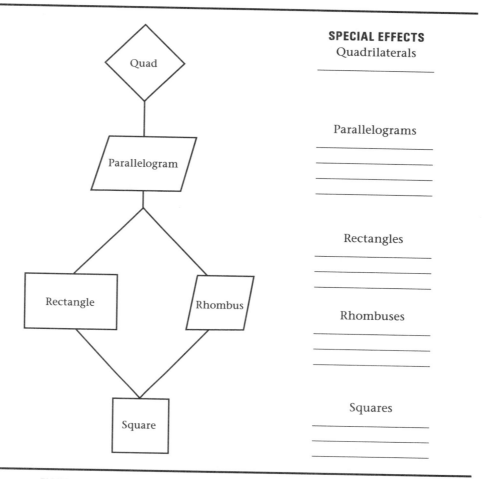

FIGURE 6.16. A flow diagram for learning geometric shapes.

pictures (diagrams of geometric shapes), and language (mathematical symbols representing the relationships). Building on prior knowledge is critical.

Individualizing Math Strategy Instruction Within Your Classroom

Many management techniques are helpful for individualizing strategy instruction within the context of a large, heterogeneous classroom or in a learning center where you see many students throughout the day.

➔ *Use math strategy notebooks with all of your students.* Math strategy notebooks are useful in classroom or small group settings for translating educational plan goals into student language. Students can identify and store their own math goals on "focus cards." They can document newly learned strategies and examples in sections

---

AREA OF PARALLELOGRAM ????

1. Prior knowledge

2. Use geoboard: What is area of *triangle*?

3. Can we turn rectangle into parallelogram?

4. Use number examples.

FIGURE 6.17. A graphic organizer for finding the area of a parallelogram.

related to their goals. For example, the notebook may contain sections on automatic recall for math facts, problem-solving strategies, and telling time. Focus cards and math rings can be stored in the students' notebooks to remind the students of their math goals and strategies. Math strategy notebooks may include some or all of the following:

- Instructional goals
- Focus cards
- Math ring in notebook pocket
- Enrichment activities
- Rules using summary clouds
- Vocabulary using three-column note strategy
- Students' custom-designed graphic organizers
- Examples of students' best work
- Individualized homework
- Curriculum extensions for gifted students

➔ *Use focus cards to help students focus on their math goals* (see Figure 6.18). Help students state their math goals in terms that are meaningful to them. For example, if they are learning to automatize multiplication facts, their focus card would highlight the goal and the strategy to achieve that goal.

➔ *Tuck math rings in the pocket of the math strategy notebook.* Math rings can be conveniently stored in the pocket of a three-ring binder

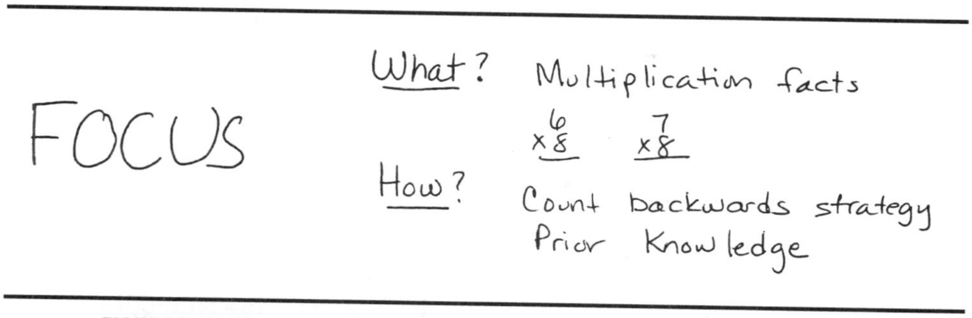

FOCUS

What? Multiplication facts

$\begin{array}{r}6\\ \times 8\\ \hline\end{array}$ $\begin{array}{r}7\\ \times 8\\ \hline\end{array}$

How? Count backwards strategy
Prior Knowledge

FIGURE 6.18. Focus cards can be used to help students define their math goals.

or coil-bound notebook. By having the math rings accessible and by experiencing daily classroom verbal drills, your students will get into the routine of looking at their math rings and practicing their math facts daily to improve their automatic recall of facts.

→ ***Enrich and extend your advanced students' mathematical thinking.*** Depending on your students' ages and your instructional goals, you can offer certain students curriculum extensions by introducing new math vocabulary, such as reciprocals and commutative property, and algebraic equations. During practice labs, these students can work independently or collectively on an ongoing interdisciplinary math and science technology project. While other students are practicing skills and strategies in practice labs, you can spend some time interacting with those students who learn quickly and would benefit from additional challenges.

→ ***Create strategy groups.*** Students are often grouped based on ability rather than the strategy they need to learn or practice. To encourage strategy use, you can form strategy groups that are flexible, homogeneous groups within a heterogeneous classroom. These groups are set up according to the math goals and strategies that your students are studying. For example, students who need math ring practice in order to automatize certain math facts may be in one group, while students who need practice learning a problem-solving strategy may be in another. Other strategy groups could be formed to work on addition facts, multiplication facts, graphic organizers for problem solving, drawing diagrams for problem solving, and working on problem-solving projects. Although all students benefit from exposure to all of these aspects of math instruction, following a full class presentation, these groups can be formed to practice specific skills and strategies.

Other factors to consider when defining groups are students' learning style strengths. By structuring time for practicing strategies (strategy time or practice lab), you will find that you have more time to interact with small groups of students while others practice and problem-solve in small groups or work individually. Using math strategy notebooks and focus cards as your guides, strategy time and practice labs that last from 10 to 20 minutes can provide an effective use of time to individualize within your classroom.

➡️ ***Set up math labs.*** Teachers commonly ask, "How can I orchestrate strategy groups and practice labs during math time?" Here is an example of how two teachers, who felt they were shortchanging the gifted students in their classes, set up math labs for students who needed strategy instruction and for others who needed more challenge. Three times a week, the teachers taught their own classes. Twice a week, the two teachers grouped the children according to skills and strategies for math lab; one of the teachers ran a math lab that challenged the students who needed curriculum extensions, while the other teacher combined students from both classes who needed more practice and reinforcement on particular skills or strategies. They planned their math instruction to occur at the same time each day so they could set up these strategy math labs. By teaming up with a teacher in this way, you can address a wider range of students' needs in a systematic way.

➡️ ***Individualize homework.*** Math labs, strategy time, or practice labs are opportune times to assign individualized homework. Some teachers like to have one core assignment for all of their students, and then they add on additional types of problems according to the strategy groupings. Other teachers offer completely different assignments depending on the math goals or strategies studied by different groups. For example, the math-fact recall group may get an assignment based on their math goal for the week, while the problem-solving project group takes home challenging problems related to their project. Some teachers have organized homework assignments using a color-coded system. For example, the students' focus cards are color-coded depending on their math goals, and two or three homework packets are color-coded to correspond to those goals. Sometimes, the teacher hands out colored construction paper to each student indicating which homework assignment he or she should take home on a particular night.

➡️ ***Individualize tests.*** Multiple forms of math assessment are available to assess what students have learned:

Selected Response
- Multiple choice
- True–false
- Matching

Short Answer
- Fill in the blank
- Label a diagram
- Respond in a few sentences

Essay
- Several paragraphs
- Concept map

Performance-Based Assessment
- On demand
- Projects
- Portfolios

Personal Oral Communications
- Student–teacher conferences
- Oral interview
- Oral presentation

Self-Evaluations
- Questionnaires on strategy use
- Student interviews
- Questions at the end of the test

Teacher Observations

Assessment is especially effective if you can select the method that will enable each student to show what he or she knows best. Many students who have language-based learning difficulties will not be able to "communicate" their newly learned math knowledge in essay or journal form. To bypass the written expressive language disability, use other formats that tap the students' strengths such as math projects, oral presentations, concept maps, or matching and true–false questions. Tests may be prepared such that all students are required to answer questions from a certain section of the test. Additional sections are provided to test progress on individual or small group goals. You may indicate by color or check mark the additional sections that you would like specific students to take. Collecting work samples (e.g., pages from math strategy notebooks that represent personal triumphs toward specific math goals) is an especially effective means of portfolio assessment. These portfolios can also be used for parent–teacher–student conferences. If you organize biweekly math labs where students are grouped according to ability on particular skills or strategies, then you can administer different tests at this time. Teachers can teach and test to homogeneous groups during math lab, and they can teach and test to heterogeneous groups during the other three periods of math during the week.

TABLE 6.2

Teaching Techniques To Address Multiple Learning Profiles

- Combine multiple representations (e.g., concrete aids with pictures and numerical symbols).
- Use colored chalk or colored markers to group similar information.
- Provide large-block graph paper to help students align numbers correctly.
- Fold math paper into quadrants to provide one space for each problem.
- Link new concepts to prior knowledge.
- Model three-column note-taking and summary boxes.
- Build in systematic routines and questioning sequences.
- Use real-life examples to make math concepts meaningful (e.g., money).
- Teach students how to estimate and to use estimation to check their work.
- Develop personal checklists for individuals to check their work.
- Balance verbal discussions with visual models and hands-on experiences.
- Use step-by-step question–answer routines.
- Teach students how to look for patterns across examples.
- Encourage students to paraphrase word problems aloud.
- Give students extra time to practice new strategies or procedures.
- Stay attuned to those students who "don't get it," and give those students on-the-spot tutorials so they can keep up with class.
- Follow up group lessons with individualized extra help sessions for those students who need it.

 Incorporate multisensory teaching techniques and strategies into your classroom presentations. Table 6.2 lists effective teaching techniques for addressing multiple learning profiles in the classroom.

 A MATH CASE STUDY

Keith was referred for a specific mathematics evaluation when he was 9 years old and in third grade. He was initially evaluated for learning problems as a repeating first-grade student. At that time, Keith was found to possess above average to superior cognitive ability. He was diagnosed with a learning disability and with ADHD–inattentive type. He demonstrated particular strengths in abstract verbal reasoning and recall of structured visual material; in contrast, weaknesses were evident in his attention to details, sequencing, automatic memory, systematic analytic reasoning, and ability to follow multistep directions. Through diagnostic math educational therapy, Keith was identified as having processing strengths in classifying and categorizing both linguistic and nonlinguistic knowledge. Furthermore, Keith's fine-motor output and visual and drawing abilities were extraordinary. On the other hand, he had significant weaknesses in analysis, memory, sequencing, and pattern completion. Keith's automatic recall for letters and numbers was poor, and complex tasks involving multiple details overwhelmed him. (See Table 6.3 for assessment findings and recommendations.)

These findings helped to explain the difficulties Keith had been experiencing in learning mathematics. His general lack of automaticity and difficulty "shifting sets" interfered with his ability to memorize math facts, represent number concepts with manipulatives, and translate words into numerical representations. Specifically, shifting between linguistic and numerical processing compromised Keith's strong logical reasoning skills. In addition, his attention deficits resulted in many impulsive responses and poor self-monitoring strategies.

Selective mainstreaming with close communication and cooperation between the classroom teacher and a special educator was recommended. In this manner, Keith would receive frequent individualized instruction and review.

Two main math goals were identified for Keith: increasing his automaticity for recalling number facts and learning systematic approaches and strategies for solving math word problems. It was recommended that Keith be given structured, multisensory, and contextual learning opportunities in mathematics. These techniques would help Keith access his logical reasoning strengths. In particular, it was suggested that Keith be encouraged to work to improve his automatic recall for math facts.

Specific instructional strategies included the identification of stratofacts and clueless facts to construct personalized fact rings, tables, and other graphic organizers. It was also recommended that Keith be taught specific structured routines to develop meaningful math problem-solving strategies. In conjunction with developing personalized visual representations of useful strategies (see Figure 6.19 for illustrations of Keith's work), it was recommended that Keith be taught to construct a math strategy notebook as a metacognitive aid and as a means of providing ongoing documentation of his developing mathematical strategies. Teaching techniques such as CSA (Miller & Mercer, 1993) were suggested to help Keith to proceed from concrete to semiconcrete to abstract mathematical reasoning. Finally, Keith's difficulties in switching flexibly between verbal and numerical representations justified the use of computational bypasses (e.g., calculators) in complex problem-solving situations.

TABLE 6.3
Case Study Findings and Recommendations

Processes	Educational Manifestations	Recommendations[a]
Strengths		
Abstract reasoning	Accurate problem solving when tasks are well structured Strengths in analyzing oral information Strong classification and categorization skills Able to apply general rules appropriately	Specify sequences for solving problems Brainstorm multiple strategies and solutions Restate problems in his own words
Visual processing	Good performance when solving visually formatted problems Artistically talented	Draw pictures of word problems Teach use of graphic organizers Color-code written information in math problems
Weaknesses		
Automatic memory	Cannot remember math facts	Math fact drill with emphasis on remembering strategies (e.g., one-up rule, doubles, math fact families) Use math strategy notebook, fact rings Use calculator and/or chart of "troublesome facts" when concentrating on word problem solutions Direct instruction in estimation and rounding Teach facts in meaningful contexts (e.g., rhymes, mnemonics) Instruction in creating procedural lists and charts Extensive spiraled instruction
Sequencing	Lacks systematic approaches to solving word problems Difficulty performing multistep procedures	Use of focus rings for problem-solving strategies Teach structured routines (e.g., RAPM)

(continues)

TABLE 6.3 *Continued.*

Case Study Findings and Recommendations

Processes	Educational Manifestations	Recommendations[a]
Flexibility	Difficulty translating words into numerical representations	Minimize reading demands Teach use of graphic organizers, tables, checklists for self-monitoring
Attention	Distractible	Preferential seating near teacher and/or away from distractions Reduce amount of text per page
	Attacks problem solving impulsively	Break down multistep directions and repeat if necessary
Self-monitoring	Does not recognize own computational errors	Create and refer to self-check lists

[a]All of the suggested instructional strategies can be integrated into the regular classroom by incorporating techniques of flexible groupings and practice labs.

Conclusion

In today's math classrooms that focus on the Principles and Standards of the National Council of Teachers of Mathematics (2000) as well as nationwide standardized tests, it is critical to meet the diverse needs of your students. An Assessment for Teaching paradigm can help you understand the multiple learning profiles of your students. At the same time, diagnostic math educational therapy (MET) can provide insight regarding how and what to teach students so that they can achieve math competence.

In math classrooms, filled with students who learn differently, teachers must continually strive toward achieving balance in instruction. Ask yourself these questions:

- Am I balancing rote instruction with meaningful problem solving?
- Am I addressing the needs of the students who are slow processors, as well as providing curriculum challenges for the mathematically gifted students?
- Am I using multisensory instruction—that is, balancing oral lecture and classroom discourse with visual models and hands-on opportunities?
- Am I balancing the teaching of math skills with the teaching of math strategies?

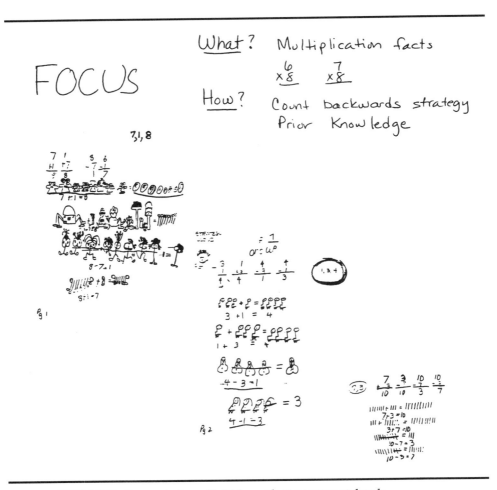

FIGURE 6.19. Excerpts from Keith's math strategy notebook.

Some students who have trouble in math classrooms have excellent quantitative skills, but they struggle in mathematics because the way in which the information is presented or tested in class taps their learning differences instead of their strengths. Other students who struggle have a great deal of difficulty in one or many areas, such as automatic recall of math facts, learning the sequence of a computational procedure, assimilating multiple processes simultaneously to solve math word problems, or understanding quantitative concepts due to lack of number sense. Students need to learn how to make decisions about which tool is best to use in the process of solving math problems: mental computation, calculators, computers, software, or pencil and paper.

Mathematics instruction must be designed to provide a balance between rote learning and meaningful problem solving. In a heterogeneous classroom where students have multiple learning profiles, students need to be taught math skills as well as math strategies. Furthermore, all students, especially those with learning problems, need to learn which strategies work best for them and when and how to apply these strategies in the area of mathematics.

Chapter 7

Strategy Use Across Content Areas

[She] provided me with so many different strategies to increase my success in the classroom and in everyday life. She taught me how to take notes that catered more to my learning style, my favorite of which is two-column notes.

—Sean, college student,
speaking about his educational therapist
and the strategies he learned for mastering content

Why Teach Strategies in the Content Areas?

Strategy instruction within the content areas is especially important during intermediate and upper grades. When students reach the fourth grade, the emphasis in classrooms shifts from learning to read to reading to learn. In addition, at each critical transition point (Grade 4, Grade 7, and onset of high school), students are expected to function more independently, and a greater emphasis is placed on complex thinking and problem-solving skills. Teachers often assume that their students have already acquired the basic reading, writing, and organizational skills necessary for success in the content areas. However, this may not be the case for students with learning difficulties; for these students, success in the content areas primarily depends on consistent, direct, and explicit strategy instruction.

Not All Students Already Know How To Learn

Because most teachers were efficient students, they may find it difficult to understand that many students with learning difficulties need explicit instruction in organizational, study, and test-taking strategies. Furthermore, whereas successful students modify their strategy use to fit academic task demands, students with learning difficulties need direct strategy instruction. For example, efficient learners employ different strategies when reading an English novel than when reading a science text. In contrast, students with learning difficulties do not automatically shift strategies to match the requirements of different assignments. Their lack of flexibility in applying strategies may impede their progress in the content areas.

Areas in Which Students with Learning Difficulties May Need Instruction	▥ Using homework assignment books or personal digital assistants for short- and long-term planning ▥ Reading specialized textbooks (e.g., biology, social studies) ▥ Reading, comprehending, and recalling novels ▥ Extracting critical information from lectures ▥ Taking notes from texts and lectures ▥ Preparing and producing research papers ▥ Preparing for and taking tests

© 2006 by PRO-ED, Inc.

Students with learning difficulties are in a state of "double jeopardy" when they enter the middle and upper grades. As they make these transitions without the basic skills or strategies upon which content mastery must be scaffolded, a gap exists between the students' skills and the curriculum demands. Unfortunately, this gap often continues to widen as students progress through the middle and high school years.

Blending Strategies with Content Areas

Through specific strategy instruction, you have the tools to enhance each student's opportunity to master the material in your course. By gaining a thorough understanding of your own teaching and learning styles, as well as the demands of your curriculum, you can effectively empower your students with the strategies they need to succeed in your class.

Strategies are best taught in context. That means you are in an ideal position to teach your students not only *what* to learn but also *how* to learn in your classroom. Helping your students to understand their preferred learning styles will also allow them to experience greater success (see Appendix B.6, Learning Style Student Survey). Remember, *make no assumptions* about the skills and strategies your students bring to your course material.

The strategies needed in each class by students with learning difficulties will depend on the following:

- Each student's profile of strengths and weaknesses
- Each student's preferred learning style
- The specific course material
- The teacher's style of instruction
- The method of assessment

Examine Your Teaching Style (see Appendix B.7)

→ *Do you present most material in lecture format?* Lectures often make up close to 50% of the instructional procedures in content-area classes at the middle and high school levels. Students with learning difficulties often have trouble understanding lectures because the information is presented through a single sensory modality.

How To Modify Your Lectures	‖ Write main points on an overhead projector or chalkboard. ‖ Give students an outline of the lecture in advance. ‖ Use graphs, charts, and pictures to illustrate key concepts.

© 2006 by PRO-ED, Inc.

→ *How much independent reading is expected of students in your class?* In many content-area classes, group discussions and tests are based on textbook reading assignments. Some students with learning difficulties may be unable to extract critical information from a textbook. Reading guides and other strategies may provide the tools these students need to comprehend and retain the information from a textbook reading assignment. (See the reading strategies section of this chapter and Chapter 4 for detailed suggestions about reading comprehension.)

Help Your Students Learn Strategies for Success	‖ Analyze the demands of your curriculum. ‖ Teach reading strategies and their application to content areas. ‖ Teach strategies for taking notes from texts and lectures.

(continues)

Help Your Students Learn Strategies for Success *Continued.*	▥ Teach study and test-taking strategies. ▥ Teach test-taking strategies and content simultaneously. ▥ Examine your grading system. ▥ Teach organization for long-term research projects. ▥ Facilitate homework completion.

© 2006 by PRO-ED, Inc.

Analyze the Demands of Your Curriculum

By analyzing your course demands, you can identify the skills necessary for success in your content-area class. In other words, it is important to understand the fit between the course material, the curriculum content, and the strategies you choose to help your students learn effectively.

➡ ***Gain a perspective on what needs to be taught.***
- *Examine your course content.*
  1. Review the amount of material needed to be taught within a chapter or lesson.
  2. Consider how best to break this down.
  3. Pace yourself relative to the slower processors who may need information conveyed in different ways.
- *Look at the kind of information students will be learning.* Factor in strategy instruction and practice time.

➡ ***Review the types of materials available for use.*** Begin by examining your textbook and supplemental materials. Textbooks continue to be an integral component of most classroom instruction. Therefore, success in the classroom often depends on a student's ability to master textbook reading assignments. Teachers and students need a thorough understanding of their textbooks. Furthermore, students need strategies for comprehending material presented in textbooks. Although the readability level of a textbook is important, many other critical components influence the selection and effective use of textbooks in the classroom. Table 7.1 outlines methods for reviewing and using textbooks. (See Ciborowski, 1992, for a textbook review form.)

Once you understand your text from the perspective of the learner, share that information with your students. Take your students through the first reading assignment as you model strategies that will help them comprehend the material. Preview important vocabulary words that students will encounter in their reading. Discuss reading assignments in advance. Integrate the textbook with strategy instruction, and you will empower your students to become independent and confident learners.

TABLE 7.1

Methods for Using Textbooks in the Classroom

Is the textbook within a readable level for the group of students you are teaching?
• Use a readability index (see Appendix A.5).

Is there a study guide that can be used in conjunction with the text?
• Use the study guide to supplement the text.
• Develop outlines or reading guides to accompany the text.

How is the text organized?
• Discuss the structure of the text with your students (e.g., table of contents, glossary, index).
• Brainstorm with them the most effective ways to handle reading assignments.
• Be explicit about clues to reading, such as the main objectives listed near the chapter title, important vocabulary words highlighted in boldface, clearly delineated sections, main ideas accented in headings or in the margins, and study questions.
• Distribute lists of important words if they are not explicitly highlighted in the text.

Are the questions at the end of the chapter good prereading tools for the students?
• Encourage the students to read the questions before they begin the reading assignment.
• Be sure to have the students use these questions with their correct answers as part of their study routine.

 Explore how students can effectively learn this material. Explain the curricular demands to your students. Students with learning difficulties are not efficient at picking up subtle clues about classroom demands. In addition, they have difficulty prioritizing. Once these students understand the strategies required to succeed in a specific class, they will be more focused, less frustrated, and more likely to experience success with the content material. If your goal is mastery of the material, give your students the clues they need to solve the mystery of learning in your classroom. Success with the material and the strategies you show students will spur their motivation in your classroom.

Teach Active Reading Strategies and Their Content-Area Application

Students with learning difficulties often have difficulty reading content material. This difficulty may be because they have poor reading strategies. The approaches that students must employ to gain meaning from text will differ slightly for each subject, because the language used to communicate concepts varies among content areas. Students with learning difficulties often struggle to vary their use of reading strategies; therefore, it is critical for these students to receive strategy instruction for reading within each content area. Specific suggestions for active reading strategies that help students interact with the written page are listed in Chapter 4.

Teach Note-Taking Strategies

The emphasis on lectures and independent reading assignments in the upper grades means that students must develop efficient note-taking strategies, which are important for all students, but particularly for students with poor organizational skills and language deficits. The most effective method for teaching note taking will differ according to the learning profile of each student. You can instruct your students in a variety of note-taking techniques within the context of your course.

Note-Taking Techniques	▥ Linear outlining techniques ▥ Two-column note taking ▥ Three-column note taking ▥ Graphic organizers ▥ Highlighting

➡ *Teach linear outlining techniques.* Linear outlining is the most commonly used method. However, many students have not received explicit instruction in outlining. Students with learning difficulties need explicit and repeated instruction and practice. Outlines help students to focus on the material.
- Begin by distributing a skeletal outline, which students complete as you lecture or as they read.
- Distribute the outline in advance so students have ample time to read it.
- Model the outlining procedure on an overhead projector.
- Allow students to compare their outlines to yours.
- Gradually fade the support as students begin to assume more responsibility for their learning.
- Emphasize the use of the outline as a study guide.

➡ *Teach two-column note taking.* This technique may be an effective strategy for students who have difficulty differentiating main ideas from details. Two-column notes are also helpful as study guides because they are formatted for self-testing (see Figure 7.1 for an example).

1. Fold a sheet of paper in half lengthwise.
2. During the lecture, the student records information on the right side of the sheet.
3. After class, the student groups like information into categories or main questions.
4. The student then records the main ideas on the left side of the paper.

FIGURE 7.1. An example of two-column notes.

 Teach Triple Note Tote (three-column note taking). This approach (Institute for Learning and Development/ResearchILD and Fable Vision, 2001) is readily adaptable to any content area and is very helpful for students who require a memory strategy for internalizing the information.

• Fold a sheet of paper in thirds or draw lines.
• Reserving the last column for strategies, label each column—for example, "Term" (first column), "Definition" (second column), and "Strategy" (third column).
• Work with students initially to help them develop simple acronyms, rhymes, associations, or cartoons to place in the "Strategy" column.
• Students can self-quiz by using the strategies as memory triggers.

➔ ***Teach students to use graphic organizers.*** Graphic organizers are especially helpful for students with strong visual–spatial skills. Examples can be found in Chapters 4 and 5 of this book.
- Use graphics to illustrate the connections among ideas so that students can visualize the concepts presented.
- Use mapping and webbing strategies (see Chapters 4 and 5).

➔ ***Teach the art of highlighting.*** Highlighting is a form that needs to be systematically taught. Many students with learning difficulties do not understand how to create shortcuts for capturing main ideas and related details.
- Demonstrate on an overhead projector how to highlight key words and important phrases in personal books and notebooks, and how to create a "telegraph" language of phrases and individual words.
- Allow students to decide what should be highlighted.
- Give out brief photocopied articles for guided and independent student practice.

➔ ***Consider modifications to traditional classroom note taking.*** For a small number of students, note taking is particularly difficult. Note taking requires listening, extracting critical information, and writing at the same time. Students with weaknesses in any one of these areas can become easily overloaded, especially when they are required to perform multiple tasks. Therefore, the following modifications are useful:
- Allow students to tape-record lectures and develop outlines from the recordings.
- Allow a student to choose a friend who will act as secretary.
- Give students copies of your lecture notes.
- Appoint one strong note-taker a month to be the scribe for weaker note-takers.
- Tape-record your lectures and allow students to borrow your tapes.

➔ ***Consider various note-taking styles.*** It is important to introduce your students to a variety of note-taking techniques. By demonstrating various possibilities, you will discover that different students prefer different methods for taking notes.
- Introduce one note-taking technique per month and provide time for practice.
- Encourage students to discuss methods they prefer to use.
- Develop templates for each method and make these available in bins.
- Permit each student to select the template that suits his or her learning style.

Teach Study Strategies

Students with learning and attention difficulties often require explicit instruction in study strategies beginning in the early grades and continuing in the later grades. Many students implicitly learn how to study, but others need explicit strategy instruction, additional support, or modifications. In fact, all students benefit from instruction in study strategies.

 Teach general study strategies. Students with learning difficulties often have trouble organizing information into a logical sequence and differentiating salient information from details. Therefore, many students with learning difficulties do not know how to study for a test and need to be taught specific strategies for each content-area class.

General Study Strategies

⫴ Make strategy cards (Institute for Learning and Development/ ResearchILD and FableVision, 2001) for vocabulary words by putting the vocabulary word and a memory strategy on one side and the definition on the back. Students can self-test by reading the vocabulary word and saying the definition aloud, using the strategy to trigger the correct answer. Using both writing and speaking is a multisensory way of reinforcing the vocabulary.

⫴ Create charts when studying detailed content. For example, timelines are useful for remembering the sequence of events in a history or social studies class. The visual aids will help to reinforce the order of the events.

⫴ Develop a key word–question–answer review sheet by dividing a paper into three columns and writing an important (key) word in the first column, a specific question in the second, and the answer in the third. The key words will help students remember the questions and answers. Again, students can self-test by answering questions aloud. The Triple Note Tote (described previously) is an effective strategy as well; use three columns for term, definition, and strategy.

⫴ Give a pretest or practice test similar to the real thing. Students can do this as an in-class exercise or as a homework assignment.

Teach use of study guides. As previously discussed, separating the main ideas from less salient details is extremely difficult for students with learning difficulties. Therefore, study guides provide helpful concrete guidance. Teacher-created study guides supply students with direction and organization for studying. (It is important for teachers to remember to use the information given to the students in the study guides when creating the tests.)

Examples of Study Guides	▥ *Questions:* If your textbook supplies helpful questions at the chapter ends, point these out to students. Otherwise, create a list of your own questions. ▥ *Vocabulary/concept lists:* These lists supply students with important terms or concepts to focus their studying. The student's job is to find information to define or describe these. The lists work especially well in science, social studies, and foreign language classes. ▥ *Graphic organizers:* Visually organized information will help students associate like ideas. ▥ *Essay questions:* Give a sampling of potential questions students will need to answer on your test as a guide. Then be sure to use some of them!

➔   *Teach ways to review notes.* Depending on their learning styles, students benefit from some or all of the following strategies.

1. Allow time during or after class for students to discuss their questions about their notes (critical for all students).
2. Encourage students to
   - rewrite their notes or make flash cards from them
   - highlight important information in the notes
   - recite notes
   - reread notes
   - tape-record and listen to notes
   - self-quiz by covering sections

Teach Test-Taking Strategies and Content Simultaneously

Students with learning difficulties frequently experience problems with tests, especially when they are timed. Problems are often identified only after frequent discrepancies are discovered between the students' high grades for in-class work and their low scores on classroom-based or standardized tests. The performance of students with learning difficulties often varies depending on the test format, which may include fill-in-the-blank procedures, matching, short answer or long essays, and standard multiple-choice formats. Students with learning difficulties often experience confusion when the test format differs from the format of the original text. The vocabulary used on the tests may also be problematic. Multiple-choice tests are particularly problematic for students with learning difficulties because of the emphasis on detecting salience, isolating critical information, ignoring less relevant details, and analyzing complex language. Furthermore, the layout of the record forms for standardized tests is often confusing, because many of these students experience spatial organization problems as well.

To prepare students for tests, while simultaneously teaching the course content, you can use some of the following approaches:

- Begin teaching test-taking strategies at the beginning of the year and reinforce them in advance of each test.
- Provide explicit study guides that describe exactly what students will be expected to know for the test. Suggestions for study guides can be found in the previous section.
- Give samples of previous tests so that students have models for the language and question types you use.
- Take your students through a practice test, demonstrating the various levels of information they will need to answer the different types of questions you may use.
- Show them how to prepare for each type of test question (e.g., review strategies for multiple choice, true/false, fill-in-the-blank, and outlining for possible essays). (Refer to the test-taking section in this chapter.)

During testing, all students could benefit from additional teacher support and modeling of test-taking strategies. Have students take a deep relaxation breath before starting. Tell them to switch pencils or pens if their minds go blank. Be certain that you have allotted sufficient time for students to complete your test. A good guideline is to *triple* the amount of time it takes for you to complete your own test.

How To Help Students During Tests	⦀ Review directions aloud. ⦀ Post specific time intervals. ⦀ Call attention to specific sections of the test and how many points they are worth. ⦀ Suggest time allotments for each section. ⦀ Encourage clarifying questions.

Tests usually fall into three categories:

- *Recognition tests:* Multiple choice, true/false, matching
- *Recall tests:* Fill-in-the-blank, list, label, diagram, define
- *Production tests:* Word problems, essays, short answer, computation

Each type of question necessitates the application of different processes or skills. A student's performance on a test will sometimes depend on the test format. By using a combination of question types, including recognition, recall, and production, you can provide opportunities for students with various learning styles to show what they know. It is especially important that students with learning disabilities (LD) and attention-deficit disorders (ADD) understand what is required to answer each type of question.

Steps Involved in Test Taking	⫼ *Test preparation:* What to do at home to study for the test ⫼ *Pre–test-taking strategies:* What to do before beginning the test ⫼ *Test-taking strategies:* What to do during the test ⫼ *Post–test-taking strategies:* What to do at the end of the test

Multiple-Choice Tests

Multiple-choice tests are the most common type of recognition tests. They require students to detect salience, isolate critical details, ignore less relevant details, analyze complex language, conform to time limits, and differentiate between similar responses. These skills are often difficult for students with LD and ADD. In addition, the spatial layouts of many multiple-choice tests are confusing for some students, because the lines of type are often close together, which can be distracting. When a separate answer page is provided, the extra step of transferring the answers can be problematic for some students who have visual–spatial, attentional, or organizational difficulties.

 Preparation Strategies for Multiple-Choice Tests. In multiple-choice tests, students are required to recognize the correct answer. Many students read only the required material, and then think that they have studied appropriately for a multiple-choice test. In fact, they have learned the material at a surface level but not to the level of recall. Answers on multiple-choice tests are often similar, which may create confusion for students who study only to the level of recognition. For these reasons, it is important to teach students how to study effectively. Some techniques for studying to the level of recall in multiple-choice tests include the following:

- Teach students to use strategies such as mnemonic devices to memorize lists, dates, and vocabulary terms.
- Remind students to answer recognition questions at the ends of chapters. Go over these with your students and discuss how the correct answer was chosen.

Model these strategies in class, present as an in-class test preparation activity, and assign these activities for homework several days in advance of the test.

→ ***Pre–Test-Taking Strategies for Multiple-Choice Tests.*** To help students with conditions such as LD and ADD to avoid feeling overwhelmed by the format and length of many multiple-choice tests, you can explicitly teach and model the following pre–test-taking strategies:

- Tell students to skim the layout of the test. Is there a separate answer sheet?
- Let students use index cards or rulers to track along if there is a separate answer sheet. Older students may wish to use their pencil as a line marker.
- Tell students to read directions carefully to find out if there is a penalty for guessing. This may not be particularly applicable in the classroom; however, points are deducted for guessing on some standardized tests.
- Alert students to important words in test items, such as, "Choose the statement that is *not* correct," "Which of the following occurred *after* 1945?" or "What is the *closest* answer to the problem 658 + 789 = ?" Tell students to underline these words when reading the question initially.
- Teach students to break down multiple-choice questions by paraphrasing each part for clarification and by crossing out unimportant information.

→ ***Multiple-Choice Test Strategies.*** Once students have completed the pre–test-taking strategies, they should be explicitly taught how to approach the actual questions and how to decide on an answer. Demonstrate use of the following strategies on a sample multiple-choice test.

Strategies for Multiple-Choice Tests

▥ Teach students to read all of the questions, answering only the ones students know first. Circle the numbers of the difficult questions that students need to think about, and return to these questions later.

▥ Teach students to read the question while covering up the answer choices. Students should first paraphrase the question stem mentally, then generate their own answer before checking the possible answer choices and choosing the best match to their original response.

▥ Because multiple-choice answers usually include a correct answer, an answer that is obviously wrong, and two answers that are close to the correct one, teach students to cross out the choice that is wrong and to use a process of elimination to help limit the number of answer choices.

▥ Tell students to notice names, dates, and places mentioned in other questions and use the information as clues to help answer more difficult questions.

(continues)

Strategies for Multiple-Choice Tests

Continued.

- ‖ Tell students to read the question-carrier phrase thoroughly with each answer to decide which one fits best. For example, consider the following question:

  The first president of the United States was
  - a. Thomas Jefferson
  - b. Susan B. Anthony
  - c. George Washington
  - d. Bill Clinton

  Read, "The first president of the United States was . . . Thomas Jefferson." Repeat this for each answer.
- ‖ Tell students to guess if they are not sure (if there is no penalty for guessing).
- ‖ Plan ahead to save time for checking answers. Lengthy tests should be given over two class periods. By making the test length realistic in relation to the allotted time, you can factor in 5 or 10 minutes for checking.
- ‖ Inform students to change only those answers that students are certain are incorrect. Otherwise, it is usually smart to stay with the initial response.

Matching and True/False Tests

Matching tests require students to recognize connected ideas. Often, these tests are formatted as two lists in which the student must find the facts or ideas that are related. True/false tests are also widely used. Statements are usually presented to students, who decide whether the fact or idea is true or false. A variation is to ask students to explain why the statement is true or false; in this way, students are required to support their answers with additional facts.

Strategies for Matching and True/False Tests

- ‖ Read all of the items first before making any decisions.
- ‖ Answer known questions first.
- ‖ For matching, count the number of items on each side to see whether each column contains the same number of items. If so, cross out choices as they are used.
- ‖ For true/false items, watch for absolute terms such as *always* and *never*. These statements are often false.

Fill-in-the-Blank and Diagram/Map Tests

Recall tests require students to remember unrelated target words, such as facts or names, and to use context clues. These tests also require strong visual memory. Fill-in-the-blank and labeling tests may be extremely difficult for students with learning difficulties who have language-based word-retrieval problems, because it is difficult for them to recall specific names or words. Often, students with word-retrieval difficulties can "talk around" a word but are unable to supply an exact label. For example, these students may provide the function or description of an object but cannot produce the specific label. To address these weaknesses, it is important to teach these students specific test-taking strategies.

➡️ *Preparation Strategies for Fill-in-the-Blank and Diagram/Map Tests.* For fill-in-the-blank exams, students need to recall specific words and details. Therefore, mnemonic devices are especially useful for students with learning difficulties. Mnemonic devices provide memory associations that help students recall important details. There are various forms of mnemonic devices, including acronyms, strategy cards, rhymes and crazy phrases, rhythms, and visual associations. An acronym used for memorizing a list could be created by using the first letter from each item to make a word or sentence (e.g., COPS uses the first letter of each proofreading step: **C**apitalization, **O**rganization, **P**unctuation, and **S**pelling). Strategy cards are useful for memorizing definitions, answers to specific questions, important names, dates, and events, or even formulas, so that students can test themselves. Effective preparation for learning precise labels on diagrams or maps requires a combination of visual, verbal, and hands-on strategies. Students benefit from preparing the labels they need to know on narrow, colorful Post-it flags. This process puts the precise words into their short-term memory for later use with long-term memory strategies. Students also need to acquire or draw a blank map or diagram of what will be tested, practice placing labels, and follow up by checking against the original that was already completed.

➡️ *Pre–Test-Taking Strategies for Fill-in-the-Blank and Diagram/Map Tests.* Recognition and recall tests are similar in that they both require a single "correct" answer. Many of the pre–test-taking strategies listed in the multiple-choice section may be employed for recall tests as well. In addition, the following suggestions are specifically applicable to recall tests.

Strategies for Fill-in-the-Blank and Diagram/ Map Tests

▌ For fill-in-the-blank tests, underline key information or context clues that will help to identify the target word.

▌ "Look around" the test for information in other sections that might relate to and trigger a target word for the fill-in statement.

▌ Read fill-in-the-blank questions completely, use recall strategies when filling in the target word, and read the completed sentence fully to self-check.

Short-Answer and Long Essay Tests

There are many similarities between short-answer and long essay tests. Both require students to understand the question, plan ideas, organize information, prioritize statements, express ideas effectively, and demonstrate mastery of the writing process. Each of these requirements may be extremely difficult for students with learning difficulties. When these demands are combined in a testing situation with the anxiety resulting from a time limit, students often become overloaded. It is essential to explicitly teach students, particularly those with memory, language, or attention issues, how to approach essay questions.

→   ***Test Preparation Strategies for Short-Answer and Essay Tests.***
Short-answer and essay tests require students to demonstrate that they have learned broad content while focusing on salient ideas. The procedures for studying for these tests can be ambiguous and abstract. Many students have difficulty organizing and studying for short-answer and essay exams.

Short-answer tests require students to respond succinctly because a limited amount of space is provided on the page. When preparing for short-answer tests, students with learning difficulties can benefit from several approaches. Long essay tests emphasize the recall of broad topics with less attention to the memorization of supporting details. However, many students with learning difficulties do not know how to find the main ideas and their related details in texts and lectures. One concrete way of finding main ideas and supporting details is the use of an active reading/note-taking strategy, such as Skim, RAP, and Map (see Chapter 4). Spiral-bound index cards come in handy for recording this information.

Strategies for Short-Answer Tests	▥ Read over the questions and answer the most familiar ones first. ▥ Mark the number of the question being skipped and return to it later on. ▥ For multiple-part questions, number the key words involved in each part. If there is only one part to the question, underline the single key word and any other directive statements. Example: <u>Name 3</u> types of tests and <u>describe</u> each (1) (2) ▥ Know ahead of time what each key word means (see Table 7.2). ▥ In the margin or on the back of the test page, briefly list cue words and phrases that will help answer the question.

(continues)

Strategies for Short-Answer Tests *Continued.*	▥ For each cue word, note an example, name, event, or other detail that supports the answer, if appropriate. ▥ To start the topic sentence, borrow from the question (e.g., Question: What were the causes of the Civil War? Topic sentence starter: The causes of the Civil War were ...).

© 2006 by PRO-ED, Inc.

 Pre–Test-Taking Strategies for Essay Tests. Because of the many facts and steps that need to be organized in an essay test, the most difficult task for many students is getting started.

1. Skim over the essay questions to determine what types of questions the test includes and how many points each question is worth.

2. Plan how much time to spend on each question. Write the allotted time next to each question.

3. Read each question carefully and analyze what is needed by doing the following:
   • Underline key words.
   • Break down multistep directions by numbering each step.
   • Develop a simple outline or "brainstorm" a list of items to include.
   • Recognize the differences among key words (e.g., *compare/ contrast, enumerate, evaluate, describe, illustrate*). (See Table 7.2 for examples of key words and their meanings.)

TABLE 7.2

Key Words Used in Essay Questions

Key Word	Ask For	Meaning
State	Everything	Describe precise terms Reproduce definition easily
Discuss	Everything	Investigate by argument Give pros and cons
Summarize	Main ideas	Give brief account of a theme or principle
Contrast	Specific characteristics	Show the differences between two or more things
Explain	Specific characteristics	Clearly state and interpret details around something
Evaluate	Give your supported opinion	Appraise the value or usefulness of something using your opinion and examples

© 2006 by PRO-ED, Inc.

Because many students with learning difficulties struggle with vocabulary, they may need explicit instruction and practice with common key words used in essay tests. A chart such as the one in Table 7.2 may assist students in understanding the sometimes subtle differences in the meanings of key words. Once students understand the question, they will be more likely to demonstrate their knowledge of the material in the essay. Here are a few examples of key words and their meanings:

- *Enumerate* the reasons for the Civil War means list the events that led to the Civil War.
- *Compare* the British system of government with the U.S. system means discuss the similarities.
- *Describe* the process of mitosis means give a detailed account in which the order of events is critical.

In addition to assistance with vocabulary, some students may need explicit structure when planning and organizing their responses to an essay question. The following are some examples of helpful organizers:

- When asked a comparison question, students can divide a page in half and list side by side the individually comparable aspects of each topic (often referred to as a T-chart). Students who learn visually may use Venn diagrams or other simple maps (see Appendix B.1).
- Provide examples or lists of the vocabulary to be used when answering an essay question. Include transition words, compare/contrast vocabulary, and content vocabulary you expect your students to know and use in their answers.
- If you want students to describe a process sequentially, allow them to use some adaptation of the process organizer displayed in Figure 7.2.

→ ***Strategies To Use for Essay Tests.*** Getting started is usually the most difficult task for students. Therefore, many of the relevant strategies are described above. The following are strategies to teach students for taking essay exams. The critical issue is to provide the structure to help students self-direct their thinking and writing.

Essay Test Strategies

▥ Encourage students to use planning time before writing to number and underline key words, make a T-chart, or jot down a mnemonic device.
▥ Encourage students to use the following essay test strategies:
　—On scrap paper, brainstorm all ideas relating to the question or make an outline or chart.

(continues)

**Essay Test
Strategies**

Continued.

—Prioritize your ideas by grouping similar information, and re-order items to be used by numbering them (1 = first priority).

—Elaborate on each item listed: describe, tell *why,* add examples, compare, and so on.

—Check off every item used.

—Refer back to initial outline many times and avoid straying from the topic by checking the essay question more than once.

—Monitor elapsed time during the test. Self-pace by writing down the time needed to complete each question.

Note to teachers: For anxious testers, focusing on the time can hinder clarity of thought. Suggest that they take a deep breath before beginning the test, use their strategies, make a positive self-statement (e.g., "I prepared well; now I'll do my best"), and work at a steady pace.

▥ Encourage students to ask themselves these questions after writing:

—Did I stay on the topic?

—Did I answer all parts of the question, using the key terms correctly?

—Does my map (list or chart) relate to the question or directions?

—Did I arrange my ideas in the order that makes the most sense?

—Have I included all of the necessary supporting details (events, examples, names, steps/stages)?

—Do I have a topic sentence or introduction?

—Did I use enough transition words so that the essay is cohesive?

—Did I proofread for common errors in grammar or spelling?

Describe a Process

Process to be described:_____

List the events in time order. _____   List the words you can use to help you
_____   move through the steps (e.g., *first, next,*
_____   *then*). _____
_____   _____
_____   _____
                                    _____

Questions to ask yourself:
1. Have you included all of the important events?
2. Are all the events in order? If not, number them in order.
3. Underline the key terms you must use in your answer.
4. Do you have enough move words to get you from beginning to end?

Use this chart to guide and remind you as you write.

FIGURE 7.2. A process organizer sheet.

Modify Test-Taking Procedures

Some students may need additional support to supplement the strategies outlined in this chapter. Consider modifying the testing time, environment, or procedures for some students.

➡️ *Give students extended time on tests.* Some students with learning and attention problems may process information slowly, which means it takes longer for them to read, write, or think about the information on a test. Therefore, time restrictions add pressure and anxiety to an already stressful situation. Many times, students may know the information but are unable to complete the test in the allotted time. In other cases, the sheer relief of knowing that they have more time helps these students to relax and complete the test within the class period.

➡️ *Change the test setting.* Permit students who are distractible or anxious to take the test in a different setting, such as the resource room or guidance office. This will free the student from distractions in a room full of people and will allow the student to read aloud and "talk" through a question without disturbing others in the classroom.

➡️ *Change the test administration procedure.* Students with reading difficulties may need to have test questions paraphrased or read aloud to them. Students with severe writing difficulties may benefit from the option to answer essay tests orally or to tape-record their answers. Access to a computer can be helpful for students who know the keyboard. Procedure modifications will enable students to demonstrate their knowledge of the material in a way that complements their strengths rather than tapping their weaknesses.

➡️ *Allow for practice and revision.* Give your students many in-class and homework opportunities to practice answering an essay question, and consider grading the students based on their improvement. Provide a template, at first, to guide students. Each time students revise their answers, they enhance their knowledge of the material while gaining the appropriate skills.

➡️ *Give the students a preview of possible questions.* Also give them charts and outlines to help them organize the material. This allows students to prepare their ideas before tests and to practice writing based on a model. This method actually facilitates review of more content than can be covered in a single exam, but beware of overloading students with an unreasonably long list of potential questions. A variation is to give students several essay questions to prepare, and then select a few questions for the test. For example, give the students five essay questions and ask only two of the questions on the actual exam.

Examine Your Grading System

In secondary school, almost half of each student's grade is based on test performance (Putnam, Deshler, & Schumaker, 1993). Some students may grasp the content of a course but lack the skills they need to demonstrate their knowledge, especially in written form. It is critical for students to understand your grading system. It is also crucial for them to have many ways to demonstrate mastery of your material. It is often helpful to include students in the decision-making process as you review different grading systems. This allows them to become more involved and to develop some ownership over the process.

When you examine your grading system, consider the following suggestions:

- *Be explicit about the grading policy.*
- *Use multilevel grading.* Grading on a multilevel basis (e.g., content, vocabulary use, spelling) allows students to know the areas in which they excel and those in which they need to improve.
- *Give credit for class participation.*
- *Evaluate students' performance in a variety of ways* (e.g., oral tests, special projects).
- *Modify your scoring system.* Not all quizzes should be based on a total of 100%. In other words, a quiz containing five questions should not have responses worth 20 points apiece. Each question is not valued as highly on the larger exam. Maintain a realistic base for the quiz questions and keep your system in line with the value of similar questions on a test (e.g., base a five-question quiz on a total of 25 points, with each question worth 5 points).

Teach Strategies To Help Students Organize for Research Projects

Research projects can seem overwhelming to students who often focus only on the final project that needs to be completed in a limited time period. It is important to emphasize the *process* of completing a research project as well as the final product. This can be accomplished by offering students phased timelines, or by breaking the written research project into manageable steps, each with its own set of guidelines, deadlines, and grades. In this manner, you can assess the students' skills at each step, track their progress, and teach specific strategies for problem areas.

| Steps for Research Projects | ‖ Locate sources
‖ Take notes
‖ Prewrite
‖ Convert prewriting to rough draft
‖ Revise into final draft
‖ Present orally |

© 2006 by PRO-ED, Inc.

➡ *Locating Sources.* Physical use of the public library is gradually becoming a lost art. Students need to be aware that a panoply of information is available to them, not only on the Internet, but also in the form of library and reference books, periodicals, magazine articles, and newspapers. Sometimes, depending on the subject matter, the text found in articles on the Web, no matter how convenient, can be overly superficial or can seem overly sophisticated and difficult to understand. A combination of Web sources, library books, and articles from microfiche should be encouraged. By middle school, students should be familiar with the workings of their school and public libraries, but all too often, they resort to the "quick click" method of Internet searches. Although valuable, if the Web becomes a primary source of information, then it is necessary to teach your students how to

- discern valid sources
- write a bibliography listing Internet sources
- identify sources that are overly simplistic and do not represent research-based reality

➡ *Note-Taking Techniques.* Many students instinctively know what is appropriate to write down for research notes. However, note taking may be very difficult for students with learning difficulties, because it combines complex skills, including reading for meaning, isolating salient ideas, paraphrasing, and organizing information. Therefore, teachers should help students learn note-taking strategies:

- Help students establish topics and subtopics.
- Check students' notes to be certain that they are recording relevant information.
- Give students practice in paraphrasing orally and in writing. Many students will not know how to restate a fact in their own words and may copy facts verbatim onto note cards. Therefore, the difference between paraphrasing (retelling in their own words) and plagiarism (copying) needs to be explicitly taught. Many students do not know the difference.

- Help students learn to organize notes in a meaningful way:
  1. Write only one note on each index card.
  2. Color-code the index cards by broad categories. Use multi-colored spiral-bound index cards for recording individual notes and color-coding by category. Perforations allow for separation later.
  3. Show students how to manipulate the cards physically to form categories and to visualize relationships between ideas.

→   ***Prewriting.*** Students benefit from prewriting steps. Options include linear outlines, semantic maps, and note card organization.

◆ *Linear outlines.* Linear outlining helps many students organize their thoughts appropriately. However, some students may feel overwhelmed by the amount of time outlining takes. Therefore, teachers could give students the option of skipping this step if they have demonstrated that they have arranged their note cards in a manner that can easily be converted into written paragraphs. Teachers may want to modify outlining in other ways to match a student's learning style—for instance, using a bulleted format with overarching headings or the topic sentence outline (see Figure 7.3).

If you would like your students to use linear outlines, it is essential to teach them how to approach and complete these outlines. Many students have never had explicit instruction in outlining and are confused by the format. Making standardized templates

---

Climates

I. **Introduction**—What is a climate?

II. **Desert**
    A. *Temperature*—A desert is a dry and hot place.
    B. *Living Things*—Specialized plants and animals live in the desert.
       1. Plants
       2. Animals

III. **Rain Forest**
    A. *Temperature*—Rain forests are often very hot and wet.
    B. *Living Things*—Plants and animals that live in the rain forest are adapted to that environment.
       1. Plants
       2. Animals

IV. **Conclusion**—What are the similarities and differences between a rain forest and a desert?

FIGURE 7.3. Example of a topic sentence outline.

available to students is helpful and will encourage them to use this prewriting tool.

An adaptation of the traditional outline is one that includes topic sentences as headings (see Figure 7.3). In this style, as in linear outlines, Roman numerals represent broad topics, and letters represent subtopics. Each letter or subtopic will become a paragraph. However, the modified version has the student substitute the subtopic with a topic sentence and include important details. This method of outlining is often helpful for students with learning difficulties, because they can see how the outline helps organize the written paper. This outline allows students to have a head start, because the topic sentences are already written.

◆ *Semantic maps.* For students who are more visual, a graphic "outline" may be more beneficial than the verbal overload of a more traditional linear outline. Semantic maps are visual representations that show how ideas are related. For a research project, similar ideas could be grouped together on the map. (Semantic maps are described in detail in Chapter 4.)

◆ *Organization of note cards.* For some students, outlining may be an unnecessary and time-consuming step. These students may benefit from grouping note cards into categories. Students can compose directly from their notes. Spiral-bound index cards that are perforated for the option of separating them are extremely useful for organizing research notes. Teaching students to cross-reference information with sources and list references in this index binder helps them maintain their research materials.

➜ *Rough Draft.* Once students have written some type of outline, they need to use this prewriting tool to begin writing a rough draft. Many students with learning difficulties do not know how to use their prewriting tools to organize their writing or how to convert this to a rough draft. Specific instruction and modeling of this process is often quite helpful. (More information about the writing process and the anatomy of a paper is provided in Chapter 5.)

➜ *Revision to Final Draft.* Many students are not aware that the revising and editing steps are an essential part of writing a research paper. Many believe that the assignment has been completed when a rough draft has been written. Explain to students what is entailed in editing and revising. Because many believe that the process refers to checking spelling and punctuation, they need to learn that an essential part of revision is reorganization of words within sentences and a more global reorganization of ideas in sentences and paragraphs.

The process of revising can also be overwhelming for a student. Therefore, it is essential to explain and model the process of revising and editing for the students. Brainstorm with your students a list of areas that need to be addressed when revising. These lists will vary depending on the grade level of the students—for example, high school students will probably have a longer, more detailed list than fourth-grade students. As mentioned previously, each step in a research paper can be examined and graded independently as a multistep grading strategy. In this manner, students will hand in rough drafts and a final copy for you to see their revisions. (For specific examples and further explanation of revision strategies, refer to Chapter 5.)

➡️ ***Oral Presentations.*** Students need to be aware that oral presentations are often organized and presented in a different manner than written projects. Many students with learning difficulties do not know how preparation and delivery of written and oral projects differ. Many students may have the conception that an oral presentation means reading a written paper aloud. Therefore, explicit guidelines or rubrics should be given to these students so that they can easily adapt the information they have learned to an oral presentation. Provide students with the following guidelines for organizing their oral presentations:

- Provide explicit, structured rubrics to help students understand your expectations.
- Teach students to write important ideas from their notes or outline onto index cards. These ideas may not be full sentences, but phrases or words to help them remember key points.
- Teach students to number and color-code index cards to help organize their presentations.
- Require the use of visual or musical aids to enhance student presentations.
- Tell students that oral presentations are often less formal than written assignments.
- Recommend that students practice repeatedly at home in front of a mirror so they can become familiar with the material and develop a style of presentation.

Facilitate Homework Completion

Chronic failure to complete homework assignments should be a red flag to teachers. A student's failure to complete assignments may reflect one or more of the following problems:

- Poor organizational skills
- Difficulty comprehending instructions
- Difficulty comprehending the material

- Inability to handle the volume of material assigned
- Boredom with mundane or unchallenging assignments
- Lack of support at home

It is critical for teachers to explore all the possible reasons why a student is not completing assignments. The strategies employed by teachers, parents, and students to remediate a homework problem will depend on the underlying cause of the difficulty.

You can encourage and facilitate homework completion using some of the following techniques.

How To Encourage Homework Completion

‖ Require assignment notebooks.

‖ Monitor students' use of the notebooks. Have them copy assignments from the board as you read them aloud at the beginning of each class.

‖ Reserve 5 minutes at the end of class for students to look at homework and ask questions to clarify assignments.

‖ Provide an example of what is expected. If necessary, do the first item of the assignment together with the class.

‖ Reduce the number of questions or problems for selected students when appropriate.

‖ Allow gifted students to complete challenging questions or projects.

‖ Start a homework club or extra help session at the end of the day.

‖ For long-term assignments, post reminders of due dates along the way, reinforce use of phased timelines, and check students' progress.

‖ Schedule parent–teacher–student conferences if necessary.

‖ Once each month, make personal phone calls to parents when students have experienced difficulties. Praise the student for consistent homework completion; voice concerns regarding incomplete assignments; and offer strategies or ideas so parents can help.

‖ Give out homework passes to those students who correctly complete 10 assignments in a row.

‖ In some cases, to increase motivation, award a bonus point for every 10 consecutive and correctly completed assignments.

‖ If possible, create a homework Web site and encourage students to check this regularly.

‖ Make parents aware of your homework Web site so that they can help their children to organize their homework schedules.

Chapter 8

Selected
Case
Studies

 CASE STUDY: JON

Jon, a bright 8½-year-old boy, was referred for evaluation in the third grade because of continuing reading problems. Jon's difficulties first became evident at the end of kindergarten when he failed to demonstrate knowledge of initial consonants. In the first grade, Jon's difficulty with sound–symbol correspondence continued. In the first and second grades, Jon received individual assistance in reading, but his skills showed little improvement and he continued to experience difficulties in reading as well as spelling.

Educational, cognitive, and linguistic testing was completed. Findings revealed a pattern of strengths and weaknesses consistent with the diagnosis of a learning disability and a mild attention-deficit disorder. Specifically, Jon showed strengths in abstract reasoning, conceptualization, and the ability to memorize meaningful information related to context. Weaknesses were evident in spatial organization, spatial memory, automatic memory, and perceptual motor output. Jon also showed a high level of distractibility and impulsivity as the assessment tasks increased in difficulty.

In the reading area, Jon's learning disability manifested in problems with word attack and decoding skills, letter reversals, and poor sight vocabulary for isolated words. Although Jon knew some sound–symbol correspondence rules, he was inefficient in applying these rules when he blended words. Furthermore, his weak automatic memory limited his ability to read sight vocabulary. However, Jon's strong conceptual reasoning allowed him to use context clues to read text. Diagnostic teaching revealed that Jon was able to recognize, generalize, and apply linguistic patterns when these were taught in a structured and systematic fashion.

Spatial memory and motor weaknesses adversely affected Jon's writing skills. Because he was not automatic with alphabet production and had difficulties with motor planning and spatial organization, writing was a laborious process. The same processing difficulties that inhibited his reading were reflected in his poor spelling. Because of these specific difficulties, Jon's written output was limited and did not reflect his creativity and strong conceptual reasoning skills.

Jon's strengths in conceptual reasoning and problem solving were evident in the mathematics area, where he showed strengths in his math problem-solving skills. However, his performance was inefficient, and his computational accuracy was compromised by his weak memory for math facts and his inattentiveness to details.

As is evident from Table 8.1, recommendations emphasized the importance of instruction that would capitalize on Jon's conceptual strengths while incorporating a significant amount of time for revision, repetition, and review of previously learned material. It was recommended that Jon receive a structured phonetic approach to teach him sound–symbol correspondence rules and syllabication to improve his reading and spelling skills. Parallel instruction in reading and spelling was recommended to help Jon recognize the interrelationships between decoding (reading) and encoding (spelling). A process writing approach emphasizing successive revisions was suggested to build on Jon's conceptual reasoning strengths while addressing his specific spelling problems. In the math area, it was suggested that Jon be taught to automatize math facts and to focus on relevant details during the computation process. It was emphasized that Jon's attentional issues should be addressed in all content areas and that he develop independent work habits by generating personalized procedure and self-check lists.

CASE STUDY: LISA

Lisa is a 9-year-old fourth-grade student who has had language, reading, and writing difficulties since kindergarten. She was evaluated during her first-grade year. Although she was diagnosed as gifted learning disabled with characteristics of attention-deficit/hyperactivity disorder (ADHD), she did not receive any special education services at that time. However, due to continued academic and social difficulties, Lisa had a complete speech and language evaluation at the end of her second-grade year. Findings indicated deficits in auditory processing, receptive language, and expressive language. She began to work with a private educational specialist weekly. Due to her ongoing learning difficulties and frustration, behavioral problems began to occur within the classroom.

At the age of 9 years, Lisa was reevaluated. Cognitive and educational testing indicated a diagnosis of a specific learning disability compounded by attentional weaknesses and social problems.

TABLE 8.1
Case Study: Jon—Grade 3

Processing Areas	Educational Manifestations	Recommendations
Strengths		
Conceptualizing information	Strong comprehension of linguistic information	*Reading* Prereading strategies: Activate prior knowledge. Use brainstorming. Use semantic mapping and webbing.
Reasoning and problem solving	Above average vocabulary skills	Use matrix. Set purposes for reading. Use active reading strategies. Encourage use of context cues.
Memorizing meaningful information in context	Strong comprehension in content areas	Model self-questioning. Use reciprocal teaching. Listen to literature read aloud by teachers, parents, audiotapes. *Writing* Process writing approach focusing on brainstorming, elaboration, and multiple edits. Teach story structure.
	Accurately analyzes and formulates solutions to math problems	*Math* Encourage estimation. Teach math skills in context of problem solving. Use manipulatives. Use reciprocal teaching.
Weaknesses		
Automatic memory	Poor word attack/ decoding	Use an integrated language arts program, which maintains consistent approach to reading, writing, and spelling.
	Computational inaccuracy Weak memory for facts	Drill math facts (games, index cards, computer programs).

(continues)

TABLE 8.1 *Continued.*

Case Study: Jon—Grade 3

Processing Areas	Educational Manifestations	Recommendations
Spatial memory	Poor spelling	Use multisensory phonetic instruction with parallel presentation of decoding and encoding.
		Use supplemental linguistic instruction emphasizing word families and rhyming.
		Maintain individual word bank.
		Develop personal editing checklist.
Spatial organization	Poor handwriting	Introduce cursive writing and ensure that Jon uses this consistently.
		Individual classroom modifications
		Teach cursive handwriting.
		Capitalize on computer technology, word processing, software for reading, and math drill.
Perceptual–motor output	Limited written output	Use a process writing approach that is structured and spiraled.
		Teach Jon to self-check using mnemonic strategies (e.g., COPS: **C**apitalization, **O**rganization, **P**unctuation, **S**entence structure and spelling).
Attention	Difficulty following multistep directions	Use preferential seating near teacher and away from distractions when necessary.
	Impulsive behavior	Break down multistep directions and repeat if necessary.
	Distractible, does not complete tasks	
	Inattentive to details	Develop individualized checklist for self-monitoring.

Strengths were evident in the area of visual memory, as well as expression of ideas in writing. Weaknesses were evident in auditory memory, expressive language, phonological processing, planning, and organization.

In the academic areas, Lisa experienced delays of approximately 1 year in reading decoding and comprehension, spelling, handwriting, writing mechanics (capitalization and punctuation), and math word problems. In the reading area, her strengths in visual memory allowed her to read sight words easily; this improved her reading fluency. However, phonological processing weaknesses resulted in laborious decoding skills, and Lisa had difficulty sounding out grade-level word lists. She also had difficulty conceptualizing main themes and recalling details about a short narrative. This was attributed to her underlying weaknesses in auditory memory and her difficulties prioritizing information. Lisa's spelling skills were also 1 year below grade level. She had trouble when spelling multisyllabic words with long and short vowel sounds. In the writing area, Lisa's stories reflected many creative ideas and a strong imagination and included a beginning, middle, and end. She did not include capitals or punctuation. Her writing was difficult to read, as many of her letters were poorly formed.

As is evident from Table 8.2, it was recommended that Lisa receive educational therapy using a systematic, structured, multisensory approach. This approach would capitalize on her visual strengths, but would also emphasize the specific strategies needed to improve her phonological awareness for spelling and decoding. It was suggested that Lisa explicitly learn the six syllable types and specific decoding rules, as well as finger-spelling techniques, which emphasize phonological segmentation.

As a result of this individualized support and other recommendations, Lisa has made great progress. Behavior within the classroom has improved as her academic frustration has decreased. Medication has helped to control her attention-deficit disorder, and she is less impulsive and more thoughtful with her work. Lisa is now performing well in her classes, and she has more positive self-esteem.

CASE STUDY: MARIA

Maria is a 12-year-old sixth grader who was referred for an evaluation because of her failure to complete classwork and homework and her poor test performance. Her teachers reported that she is extremely distractible in class and that she disrupts others. These problems were first noted in kindergarten and have continued through the years. A number of trials of stimulant medication therapy have been initiated in the past, with little success.

TABLE 8.2

Case Study: Lisa—Grade 4

Processing Areas	Educational Manifestations	Recommendations
Strengths		
Receptive language	Uses mature vocabulary while writing and speaking	Prewriting—brainstorm lists of words.
Creative ideas for written expression	Imaginative and creative ideas in writing	Write for content first. Separate grades for content and mechanics.
Visual memory	Good at reading sight words	Further develop sight vocabulary based on critical concepts in class.
Weaknesses		
Auditory memory	May not recall information presented orally Trouble following multi-step oral directions	Needs both written and oral directions.
Expressive language	Slow and imprecise when responding in class	Alert Lisa in advance of being called on so she has time to formulate her oral responses. Use semantic mapping and outlining for prewriting.
Phonological processing	Difficulty decoding Difficulty analyzing words Difficulty spelling	Use multisensory approach including instruction in syllable types and specific decoding rules. Use finger-spelling.
Organization of language	May not recall information obtained through reading Difficulty conceptualizing main themes and recalling details about narratives and text	Teach a structured, systematic, multisensory approach to reading comprehension. Teach visualization and chunking strategies. Use reciprocal teaching.

© 2006 by PRO-ED, Inc.

The assessment included educational, cognitive, and linguistic testing, as well as a review of Maria's developmental history. Findings were consistent with the diagnosis of ADHD. Maria demonstrated strengths in verbal and nonverbal problem-solving and reasoning abilities. Short-term memory skills were strong.

Weaknesses were evident in automatic memory and long-term memory. Maria also used poor self-monitoring abilities and showed limited attention to details. Organizational difficulties occurred frequently. Some areas of language were also weak, including word-retrieval skills, vocabulary knowledge, and the understanding of inferential and metaphoric language. However, when language was more literal, her receptive and expressive language skills were age appropriate.

Educational testing indicated that Maria had acquired grade-appropriate academic skills. In the area of reading, Maria displayed grade-appropriate skills in word recognition, decoding, and general comprehension. However, poor attention contributed to her difficulty in keeping her place while reading, and she often skipped over words or lines. In addition, she had difficulty with vocabulary. In the area of writing, Maria's strengths in abstract reasoning were reflected in her ability to generate creative and meaningful themes. Attentional weaknesses contributed to her difficulties prioritizing and to her inconsistent use of punctuation, sentence structure, and spelling. In the area of math, Maria exhibited a good understanding of concepts and word problems, consistent with her strong reasoning abilities. Weak automatic memory was reflected in her hesitation with math facts. She made many errors typical of students with attention-deficit disorders, including computational errors when she computed multistep calculations, poor self-monitoring, and inattention to details (e.g., decimals, dollar signs).

Maria's ADHD also manifested in the social area. Maria had difficulty establishing and maintaining friendships, in part due to her difficulties inhibiting her comments. She was seldom able to anticipate the consequences of her behavior. As a result, her self-confidence was diminished. She made many negative comments about herself and her work. She described many worries and reportedly exhibited somatic signs of tension (e.g., frequent headaches, nail-biting).

As is evident from Table 8.3, it was recommended that Maria receive numerous classroom modifications to accommodate her ADHD so that she could begin to experience success. Educational therapy services were recommended to help her develop effective educational strategies. Psychotherapy was also recommended to address social–emotional issues. Specific recommendations are outlined in the table.

(text continues on p. 164)

TABLE 8.3
Case Study: Maria—Grade 6

Processing Areas	Educational Manifestations	Recommendations
Strengths		
Abstract reasoning	Good understanding of concepts	Preview concepts at the beginning of each lesson or unit of study.
	Good overall reading and language comprehension	Teach prereading and prewriting strategies.
	Good math problem-solving ability	Relate new information to that which is known.
		Present information in meaningful contexts.
		Keep class discussions lively and relevant.
		Include hands-on, experiential projects and visual aids whenever possible.
Short-term memory	May grasp concepts initially but forgets important facts and details over time	Teach recall strategies emphasizing mnemonic cues (e.g., acronyms, visual associations).
Weaknesses		
Automatic memory	Hesitates on math facts	Determine which memory facts are "stratofacts" or "clueless facts."
		Develop strategies for clueless facts before building up speed.
		Encourage use of computer games with appropriate facts at home or at school.
Long-term memory	Due to retrieval difficulties, may have problems accessing prior knowledge	Activate prior knowledge through brainstorming and discussion.

(continues)

TABLE 8.3 *Continued.*
Case Study: Maria—Grade 6

Processing Areas	Educational Manifestations	Recommendations
Attention	Distracted by external and internal stimuli	Use preferential seating.
	Inattentive during lecture	Develop a behavioral checklist targeting 45 key behaviors each day.
	Talks in class	
	Disrupts other students	
	Rarely participates	Set goals for daily and weekly performance.
Self-monitoring	Inconsistent use of punctuation, sentence structure, and spelling	Model the use of active strategies and self-instructions while performing complex math and writing assignments.
	Calculation errors in math, does not check her work or include details (e.g., decimals, dollars signs), confuses operational signs	Develop checklists for solving math processes or editing written work (e.g., FOIL, COPS).
	Loses her place in reading when comprehension falters (e.g., skips words, lines)	Teach active reading strategies, especially clarifying and self-questioning.
Organization	Forgets to bring assignments and materials to and from school	Have all assignments recorded in an assignment notebook, which is signed by teacher and parent.
		Develop a notebook/folder system for storing completed or assigned work papers.
		Develop a system for cross-checking materials going to and from school (e.g., peer assistance, use of icons).
	Has difficulty completing long-range assignments	Break the assignment into manageable units.
		Develop a study plan with goals and timelines.
		Check at various points along the process.

(continues)

TABLE 8.3 *Continued.*

Case Study: Maria—Grade 6

Processing Areas	Educational Manifestations	Recommendations
Organization (*continued*)	Messy work space	Provide assistance with organization of locker at school and work space at home. Allow a few minutes each day for reorganization. Encourage parents to do the same for work space at home.
	Difficulty prioritizing ideas	Teach organizational strategies for reading and writing, including semantic mapping, two-column note taking, prewriting strategies.
Vocabulary knowledge	Misses key information when reading	Preview vocabulary before a lesson or unit of study. Develop a personalized word bank. Teach recall strategies (e.g., key word) and structural properties. Teach strategies for analyzing word meanings through context.

© 2006 by PRO-ED, Inc.

 CASE STUDY: SAM

Sam is a 14-year-old eighth grader who has been experiencing considerable difficulty with reading and writing. Sam's problems were evident from an early age, and special needs services were provided. However, little progress was made. At the age of 9 years, an evaluation resulted in the diagnosis of a learning disability and recommendations for intensive remediation. At age 10, Sam began to exhibit behavior problems, including aggressive behaviors and difficulty with peers. Sam's lack of progress led to diminished self-confidence, and he showed a pattern of "learned helplessness." He demonstrated limited motivation and had considerable difficulty completing tasks, thus falling further behind. He began to socialize with a "tough" crowd at school and exhibited numerous discipline problems.

At age 13, Sam was reevaluated. Educational, cognitive, and linguistic testing confirmed the diagnosis of a language-based learning disability. Sam demonstrated strengths in his reasoning ability, range of knowledge, understanding of part–whole relationships, and visual memory. He performed best on tasks that provided an overt structure. Weaknesses were evident in the areas of receptive and expressive language, auditory processing skills, organization, fine-motor skills, and phonological awareness.

In academic areas, Sam demonstrated relative strengths in the area of math, with his performance falling solidly in the average range. It appeared that Sam's strong reasoning abilities and understanding of part–whole relationships contributed to his success with math. He also benefited from the highly structured nature of mathematical processes. In the area of reading, Sam demonstrated variable performance in decoding skills. Although gains had been made over the years, he still made many errors and lacked automaticity. Sam's reading comprehension was also variable. He showed strengths on tasks that capitalized on reasoning abilities and minimized memory. He showed weaknesses on tasks that required organization of verbal material and integration of details. In the area of writing, Sam's fine-motor weaknesses made writing a slow, arduous process. Spelling skills were problematic, due to his weaknesses in phonological awareness. Sam's written expression lacked thematic continuity due to problems with language and organization. Additional language weaknesses were reflected in his use of simple sentence structures and immature vocabulary.

A wide range of educational recommendations were introduced for Sam (see Table 8.4). Since he began to receive intensive remediation and classroom modifications, he has begun to make significant strides in his academic work. His academic successes have motivated him to become a more active participant in the learning process. This increased motivation has fostered a positive attitude and improved self-confidence. His behavior has also improved, and he rarely gets into trouble. He is presently alert and attentive in class, and completes his work on time.

CASE STUDY: AMY

Amy is a 15-year-old ninth-grade student who is motivated and works hard in every class. Despite her effort and positive attitude toward school, Amy has earned low grades in every subject except

TABLE 8.4
Case Study: Sam—Grade 8

Processing Areas	Educational Manifestations	Recommendations
Strengths		
Verbal and nonverbal reasoning	Understands complex math concepts when these are presented in a structured way	When introducing a new math concept, develop the concept through use of manipulatives and/or visual representations *before* presenting the computational process.
Understanding of part–whole relationships	Benefits from instructional strategies with visual–spatial features	Use graphic organizers/ semantic mapping when introducing language concepts, including content-area information.
Visual memory	Understands and remembers best when information is presented visually	Teach recall strategies that emphasize visual features (e.g., imagery, visual associations). Use visual aids whenever possible.
Range of knowledge	Has a wide variety of experience and knowledge of the world around him	Engage in prereading and prewriting activities to activate prior knowledge and set purposes for reading. Record these ideas on a semantic map and integrate with new information.
Weaknesses		
Receptive and expressive language	Often misinterprets directions Poor reading comprehension Limited written output, simple sentence structure	Check with him periodically to ensure that he has grasped the directions. Encourage him to request help when needed and to decrease his dependence on teacher-initiated checks.

(continues)

TABLE 8.4 *Continued.*

Case Study: Sam—Grade 8

Processing Areas	Educational Manifestations	Recommendations
Receptive and expressive language (*continued*)		Use process writing approaches. Use vocabulary building strategies. Use prereading and prewriting strategies to emphasize vocabulary and language enrichment. Use semantic mapping for prewriting.
Auditory memory	Weak spelling skills	Teach Sam spelling rules. Use mnemonics for checking his spelling. Use individualized spelling checklists.
Fine motor skills	Writing slow and labored	Encourage Sam to use a word processor to bypass the writing task.

mathematics. Her teachers reported that she has had problems with reading rate, comprehension, and vocabulary. Amy's struggles with reading began in the first grade. An evaluation showed that Amy had a 40-point discrepancy between her Verbal and Performance scores on the *Wechsler Intelligence Scale for Children–Third Edition*. In elementary school, Amy received intermittent special education services in reading and speech. Currently, Amy is being tutored in history by an older student. Educational, cognitive, and linguistic testing confirmed the presence of a language-based learning disability.

Results of the assessment indicated Amy's very weak receptive and expressive language skills. In particular, her vocabulary and use of syntax were poorly developed. Consequently, although she may have understood concepts, she did not communicate effectively in tests or papers. Writing papers was especially difficult for Amy, because she was required to organize and rephrase material she had not fully comprehended. Amy also exhibited weaknesses in auditory memory and problems with information retrieval. Because of her auditory memory weaknesses, Amy did not retain information consistently. Her reading was slow and her

TABLE 8.5
Case Study: Amy—Grade 9

Processing Areas	Educational Manifestations	Recommendations
Strengths		
Nonverbal reasoning	Readily and accurately completes mathematics problems	Provide classroom accommodations. Provide visual supports for lecture classes.
Visual memory	Retains information more easily when it is presented visually	Photocopy notes. Allow untimed tests.
Weaknesses		
Auditory memory	Spends time studying but does not retain the material May not consistently re-call information pre-sented in lecture format	*Reading* Link new information with previous knowledge. Contextualize to help with meaning.
Receptive language and vocabulary	Has difficulty deriving meaning from written or spoken language Struggles to understand concepts presented auditorially	View a film before reading. Use active reading strategies. Use semantic mapping and webbing. Use highlighters: blue = main idea, red = details. Use margin notes.
	Has difficulty drawing inferences May miss metaphoric expressions	Use Skim, RAP, and Map. Use two-column notes. Draw pictures of metaphoric expressions. Use imagery.
Expressive language and word retrieval	Problems writing papers Slow and imprecise when responding orally in the classroom	*Vocabulary* Use VOCAB-LIT with drawings. Use key words. *Writing* Prewriting—Make authority inventory. Use semantic mapping. Use revision strategies: color code, peer work.

comprehension weak. Amy displayed numerous strengths in visual–perceptual functioning, nonverbal reasoning, and memory. These strengths were apparent in math.

As is evident from Table 8.5, it was recommended that Amy learn strategies to enhance her reading comprehension and retention of material. It was also suggested that she be taught strategies for organizing and monitoring her written work.

Appendix A

Helpful Tools

Appendix A.1

BrainCogs

Thirteen BrainCogs strategies (Institute for Learning and Development/ResearchILD and FableVision, 2001) are anchored in five critical cognitive processes: remembering, organizing, prioritizing, shifting, and checking. Students learn simple definitions of these processes, analyze their own learning preferences, and learn strategies that match their learning styles. They also learn to use metacognitive prompts that help them to understand and use these strategies flexibly.

Metacognitive Prompts
- *What* is the definition of the strategy?
- *When* is the strategy most helpful?
- *How* should the strategy be used?

The Cognitive Processes

1. *Remembering:* Cementing information into your brain
   - Remembering information on a short-term and long-term basis
   - Using multimodal approaches to learn

   BrainCogs strategies:
   - *Crazy phrases*—Make up a wacky sentence to help remember names, places, or events in a specific order.
   - *Acronyms*—Make up a real or nonsense word in which each letter is the first letter of something you are trying to remember.
   - *Cartoons*—Draw a picture that helps you remember key information.

2. *Organizing:* Juggling and sorting important information
   - Gathering important books, notes, and quizzes
   - Planning work time
   - Color coding
   - Keeping track of deadlines

BrainCogs strategies:
- *Strategy cards*—Create index cards with a question and a strategy for remembering the answer on one side, and the answer on the other.
- *Triple Note Tote* (three columns)—Create a chart to use for taking notes from a textbook.
- *Mapping and webbing*—Create maps and webs to organize main ideas and supporting details.

3. *Prioritizing:* Figuring out what is most important
- Sorting and ordering information to stress what is most important
- Getting "unstuck"
- Getting started
- Managing time
- Teachers as "human highlighters"

BrainCogs strategies:
- *1-2-3 Blastoff!*—Learn to relax, read carefully, and begin a test.
- *Red flag*—Mark test questions that are too hard to answer right away.
- *ANN E. BOA*—Use this acronym to help find seven tricky words in test questions.

4. *Shifting:* Looking again in a brand new way
- Critical for reading comprehension, writing, and math problem solving
- Shifting from main ideas to details
- Approaching the same information from different viewpoints
- Interpreting test questions in different ways

BrainCogs strategies:
- *Shifty words*—See more than one meaning for a word by shifting the accent or making nouns into verbs or vice versa.
- *Shifty images*—Find the meaning of a word by looking for clues in the surrounding words.

5. *Checking:* Recognizing and fixing the kinds of mistakes you make
- Knowing personal errors
- Finding personal errors

BrainCogs strategies:
- *Your personal checklist*—List the usual mistakes you tend to make on a test.
- *RE-view*—Learn to change your focus at the end of a test so checking your answers is more successful.

The BrainCogs strategies are summarized in Figure A.1, The Five Cogs, which may be copied and distributed for student use.

The Five Cogs

remembering

- **Crazy phrases**—Make up a wacky sentence to help remember names, places, or events in a specific order.
- **Acronyms**—Make up a real or nonsense word in which each letter is the first letter of something you are trying to remember.
- **Cartoons**—Draw a picture that helps you remember key information.

organizing

- **Strategy cards**—Create index cards with a question and a strategy for remembering the answer on one side, and the answer on the other.
- **Triple Note Tote (three columns)**—Create a chart to use for taking notes from a textbook.
- **Mapping and webbing**—Create maps and webs to organize main ideas and supporting details.

prioritizing

- **1-2-3 Blastoff!**—Learn to relax, read carefully, and begin a test.
- **Red flag**—Mark test questions that are too hard to answer right away.
- **ANN E. BOA**—Use this acronym to help find seven tricky words in test questions.

shifting

- **Shifty words**—See more than one meaning for a word by shifting the accent or making nouns into verbs or vice versa.
- **Shifty images**—Find the meaning of a word by looking for clues in the surrounding words.

checking

- **Your personal checklist**—List the usual mistakes you tend to make on a test.
- **RE-view**—Learn to change your focus at the end of a test so checking your answers is more successful.

FIGURE A.1. The Five Cogs represent different cognitive processes for learning and studying. There are a total of 13 strategies taught within the program, grouped according to the different cogs. *Note.* Reprinted from BrainCogs: The Test Taking Survival Kit [Computer software], by Institute for Learning and Development/ResearchILD and FableVision, 2001. Copyright 2001 by ILD/FableVision. Reprinted with permission.

Appendix A.2

Spelling Rules

F, L, S Generalization

Short-vowel words of one syllable ending in the sounds /f/, /l/, or /s/ end with **–ff, –ll**, or **–ss.**

Examples:

fluff	will	miss
staff	spill	class
off	spell	fuss

K/ CK/ KE Generalization

If a word ends in the /k/ sound, the spelling rules are as follows:

- After a short vowel, use *ck*.
- After a consonant or double vowel sound (oo, ee), use *k*.
- After a long vowel, usually use *ke*.

Examples:

ck	k	ke
shack	shark	shake
back	bark	bake
black	bask	rake
pick	perk	pike
luck	mask	poke

CH/TCH Generalization

If a word ends in the /ch/ sound, use the following spelling rules:
- After a short vowel, use *tch*.
- After a consonant, long vowel, or double vowel sound, use *ch*.

Examples:

tch	ch
catch	starch
pitch	pinch
fetch	birch
itch	bench
match	munch
	ouch
	pouch

Some exceptions: much/such, ostrich

GE/DGE Generalization

If a word ends in the /ge/ sound, use the following spelling rules:

- After a short vowel, use *dge*.
- After a consonant, long vowel, or double vowel sound, use *ge*.

Examples:

dge	ge
dodge	singe
badge	barge
ridge	urge

1-1-1 Doubling Rule

The rules for doubling a consonant before a suffix are as follows:

- For *one*-syllable words that end in *one* consonant after *one* vowel, double the final consonant before a suffix beginning with a vowel.

Examples:

big	→	bigger
run	→	running
fish	→	fishing
spark	→	sparked

- Do not double the consonant before a suffix beginning with a consonant.

OI/OY Generalization

The rules for spelling the /oi/ sound follow:

- The /oi/ sound in the beginning or middle of a word is usually spelled *oi*.
- The /oi/ sound at the end of a word is usually spelled *oy*.

Examples:

oi	oy
oil	boy
spoil	destroy

Y Rule

Change *y* to *i* when adding *any* suffix unless *y* is part of a diphthong.

Examples:

change *y* to *i* + suffix	*y* in diphthong + suffix
cry + ed = cried	play + ed = played
dirty + est = dirtiest	play + ful = playful
lonely + ness = loneliness	volley + ing = volleying
	employ + ment = employment

Exception: Do not change *y* to *i* when the suffix begins with *i* (e.g., baby + ish = babyish).

Silent *E* Rule

For words ending in silent *e,* use the following rules:

- Drop the *e* before a suffix beginning with a vowel.
- Do not drop the *e* before a suffix beginning with a consonant.

Examples:

    hope   hoping   hopeful

OU/ OW Generalization

For words with the /ou/ sound, use the following spelling rules:

- At the beginning or middle of a word, use *ou.*
- At the end of the word, use *ow.*

Examples:

ou	ow
out	brow
bound	plow
counter	cow

- If the word ends in an /l/, /er/, or /n/ that is preceded by the /ou/ sound, use *ow.* A mnemonic to help remember this is "lern." (Teach this rule only to older or more capable students.)

Examples:

growl	flower	brown
howl	power	clown

Note. Material in this appendix has been adapted from "The Orton–Gillingham Approach," by J. Orton, 1966, in J. Money (Ed.), *The Disabled Reader: Education of the Dyslexic Child* (pp. 119–146), Baltimore: Johns Hopkins Press.

Appendix A.3

Decoding Scope and Sequence

- ☐ Recognizes that printed materials provide information
- ☐ Knows how to handle a book and turn the pages
- ☐ Identifies front and back covers and title page of a book
- ☐ Recognizes that print moves left to right across the page and from top to bottom
- ☐ Identifies uppercase letters
- ☐ Identifies lowercase letters
- ☐ Knows the order of the alphabet
- ☐ Recognizes that written words are separated by spaces
- ☐ Recognizes that sentences in print are made up of separate words
- ☐ Knows how to rhyme
- ☐ Knows that there is a link between letters and sounds
- ☐ Identifies beginning sounds of words
- ☐ Identifies ending sounds of words
- ☐ Identifies medial sounds within words
- ☐ Manipulates syllables to create new words orally
- ☐ Manipulates sounds to create new words orally
- ☐ Identifies consonant names
- ☐ Identifies consonant sounds
- ☐ Identifies vowel names
- ☐ Defines a syllable
- ☐ Identifies short vowel sounds
- ☐ Defines a closed syllable
- ☐ Decodes words with short vowels
- ☐ Divides and decodes VC/CV words
- ☐ Identifies digraphs
- ☐ Decodes words with digraphs
- ☐ Identifies long vowel sounds
- ☐ Identifies vowel–consonant–*e* sounds
- ☐ Defines vowel–consonant–*e* syllables
- ☐ Decodes vowel–consonant–*e* words
- ☐ Divides and decodes VC/CCV and VC/CCCV words
- ☐ Defines open syllables

- ☐ Decodes open syllables
- ☐ Divides V/CV and VC/V words
- ☐ Identifies *ing, ang, ong, ung, ink, ank, onk, unk, ild, ind, old* word families
- ☐ Decodes instructed contractions
- ☐ Identifies root words
- ☐ Identifies suffixes (e.g., *able, ish, ious*)
- ☐ Identifies the plural form of given words
- ☐ Identifies the past tense of given words
- ☐ Identifies prefixes (e.g., *dis, un, pre*)
- ☐ Understands the meanings of prefixes (e.g., *pre* means "before," *un* means "not")
- ☐ Identifies *r*-controlled sounds
- ☐ Defines *r*-controlled syllable
- ☐ Decodes *r*-controlled words
- ☐ Identifies vowel diphthong sounds
- ☐ Defines vowel diphthong syllables
- ☐ Decodes words containing diphthongs
- ☐ Identifies *–le* sounds
- ☐ Defines *–le* syllables
- ☐ Decodes words containing *–le* syllables
- ☐ Divides V/V words
- ☐ Uses context clues to help decode unfamiliar words
- ☐ Uses a dictionary to look up correct spelling or definition

Note. Adapted from Eagle Hill School, Greenwich, CT.

Appendix A.4

Spelling Scope and Sequence

- ☐ Uses sound–symbol association
- ☐ Uses one–letter representations for words
- ☐ Uses invented spelling
- ☐ Represents sounds by more than one letter or group of letters
- ☐ Spells CVC words
- ☐ Uses fingerspelling (e.g., identifies sounds by putting one finger down for each sound)
- ☐ Uses *f, l, s* generalization
- ☐ Uses *k/ck/ke* generalization
- ☐ Uses *ch/tch* generalization
- ☐ Uses *ge/dge* generalization
- ☐ Uses 1-1-1 doubling rule
- ☐ Spells vowel–consonant–*e* words
- ☐ Spells these word-family words: *–ing, –ang, –ong, –ung, –ink, –ank, –onk, –unk*
- ☐ Spells these word-family words: *–ild, –ind, –old, –ost*
- ☐ Adds the following suffixes successfully: *ed* (as in *rented*), *ing, s, est, er, y, ly*
- ☐ Uses *oi/oy* generalization
- ☐ Uses *y* as a vowel
- ☐ Uses *y* rule
- ☐ Spells these word-family words: *–ire, –ain, –igh*
- ☐ Adds the following suffixes successfully: *es, ed* (as in *sailed*), *ness, ment, ish*
- ☐ Uses silent *e* rule
- ☐ Uses *ai/ay* rule
- ☐ Uses *ou/ow* generalization
- ☐ Adds the following prefixes successfully: *un, mis, dis*
- ☐ Adds the following suffixes successfully: *less, ful, age*
- ☐ Spells words ending in *tion* and *sion*
- ☐ Spells words ending in *ture*
- ☐ Spells words ending in *le*

Note. This scope and sequence list is adapted from Eagle Hill School, Greenwich, CT. See Appendix A.2 for descriptions of spelling rules.

Appendix A.5

Readability Statistics

Fry Readability Graph

Fry Graph for Estimating Reading Ages (Grade Level)

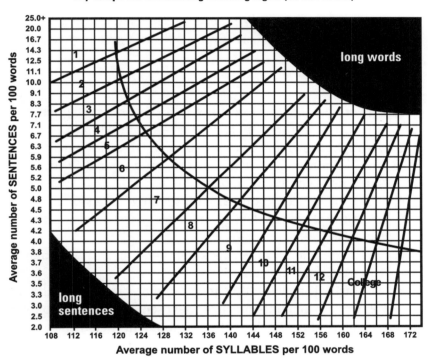

Note. From *The Reading Teacher's Book of Lists* (2nd ed.), by E. B. Fry, J. E. Kress, and D. L. Fountouki-dis, 2000, Paramus, NJ: Prentice Hall. Reprinted with permission.

Directions

1. Randomly select three 100-word passages from a book or article. Count exactly 100 words starting with the beginning of a sentence. Do not count numbers. Do count proper nouns. Mark the beginning and end points.
2. Count the number of sentences in the 100 words, estimating the length of the portion of the last sentence to the nearest 1/10th.
3. Count the total number of syllables in the 100-word passage. Use a hand counter, or simply put a mark above every syllable in each word in the marked passage and then count the marks.

4. Plot the average number of syllables and the average number of sentences per 100 words on the graph to determine the approximate grade level of the material.
5. Choose more passages per book if great variability is observed and conclude that the book has uneven readability.

Note. Few books will fall into the solid black area, but when they do, grade level scores are invalid.

Flesch-Kincaid Readability

An alternative readability procedure, the Flesch-Kincaid, is incorporated into many word processing software systems (e.g., Microsoft Word XP).

Directions
1. On your word processor, either type in or select the sample of text that you want to check for readability level.
2. Highlight the text if it is a section of a larger document.
3. On the Tools menu, click "Options," and then click the "Spelling & Grammar" tab.
4. Select the "Check grammar with spelling" check box.
5. Select the "Show readability statistics" check box, and then click "OK."
6. On the standard toolbar, click the "Spelling and Grammar" icon (ABC with checkmark).
7. Word will display spelling and grammar suggestions, and as you work through them, click "next sentence" until you reach the end of the selection. The program will then display the reading level of the document and other information.

Appendix A.6

Mining for Topics

Things I know and care about

Grades 2–6

- Who are the special people in your life? Mom, Dad, Grandmother, Grandfather? Brother, Sister, Uncle? Other? Write them down.
- Are there special things you do together? List them.
- Special places that you go? Family fun that you remember?
- What are some of the things that excite you about your family?
- Do you have a special friend? What do you do together?
- What do you like to do in your spare time? Favorite games? Hobbies? Collections?
- Have you ever taken a really great trip? Did something funny happen? Something scary? Something exciting?
- Have you ever seen anything unusual?
- What is the funniest thing that ever happened to you?
- Do you remember a time when your feelings were really hurt? When you were embarrassed?
- What makes you sad? Afraid? Very glad? Laugh?
- Have you ever been really lonely, with no one to play with?
- What are some of the things that bug you?
- Do you have a pet? More than one? How do you care for your pet? Have you ever lost a pet?
- What are you very good at? Some kids are good at a sport. Some are very good at drawing or making people laugh. Some are very good at being kind and thoughtful.
- Think of something you do very well.
- What are your favorite foods? Favorite possessions?
- Do you have a special place that you like to go to by yourself? Some kids like to lie on pillows in their closets. Some like to sit or lie on large rocks.

- Do you know a lot about something: Skateboarding? Riding a scooter? Bike tricks? Tools, cars? Books? People? Cooking?
- What is the best thing about school? The worst?
- Are there some holidays that you celebrate in special ways? Birthdays?

Note. Developed and adapted by Jacqueline Finn, educational consultant, Worcester, MA.

Sample Report: Diagnostic Math Educational Therapy Report

Student's Name: Alicia Edwards
Date: February 11, 2005
Age: 12 years 11 months
Diagnostic Educational Therapy Sessions: Approximately once/week July 2004–present
Educational Therapist: Joan Steinberg, MEd

Reasons for Referral

Alicia is in seventh grade at Pine School. She was referred for educational therapy by her parents who were concerned about Alicia's progress in math. They were interested in assessing Alicia's achievement in math and in providing Alicia with educational therapy sessions to help her progress academically.

Background Information

Alicia has attended the Pine School since third grade. She was initially diagnosed with a learning disability when she was in second grade and she participated in a team evaluation. Her second-grade results on the Wechsler Intelligence Scale for Children–Third Edition indicated that she had average to low average cognitive abilities (VIQ 87, PIQ 96, FSIQ 90). Relative strengths were observed in visual–spatial processing. Weaknesses were observed in verbal reasoning, arithmetic reasoning, and her general fund of information. Alicia also displayed difficulty when asked to process complicated visual information. The examiner noted that it was sometimes difficult to determine whether Alicia knew information but would not risk an answer, or whether she really did not know the information.

Academic testing conducted as part of the initial assessment indicated that Alicia's reading was at the 4th percentile, at the 1.2 grade level equivalent. Her math was assessed by administering the Math Applications and

Math Computation subtests of the Kaufman Test of Educational Achievement. She achieved a standard score of 76, which placed her at the 4th percentile overall for math. The math evaluator, Ruth Sampson, noted that Alicia required considerable time to formulate answers, and that she needed repetition of the questions. As a result of this evaluation, Alicia began to receive after-school tutoring services. Her parents made the decision to send her to the Pine School for third grade, so she could obtain more intensive special education services. Reportedly, Alicia has made slow but steady progress in reading at Pine School. Mrs. Edwards was interested in evaluating Alicia's mathematical achievement and in obtaining recommendations that would assist Alicia in continuing to develop math skills.

Observations

Alicia has come to educational therapy sessions willing to work hard. She has enjoyed math games, especially those using the computer. She has responded best to multisensory activities that used manipulative materials and drawings to illustrate concepts. Alicia's response style is slow, and she requires repetition and reteaching for retention.

Tests Administered

Survey of Problem Solving Skills
Survey of Educational Skills
Key Math Test
Informal math assessment

Automaticity

An informal assessment of Alicia's automatic knowledge of multiplication facts indicated that she could "skip count" by 5s and 10s, and had partial knowledge of skip counting by 2s, 3s, 4s, and 6s. She articulated strategies she had been taught to remember the next number in the sequence. For example, for skip counting by 6, she knew that her age (12) was followed by someone else's age (18) and then by the number of kids in a class (24). However, when asked a math fact, such as 2×4, she could not answer.

Concepts

Initially, Alicia demonstrated understanding of place value through the thousandths place. With instruction, she used Digiblocks to demonstrate her understanding of place value, addition, and subtraction. She was not able to estimate sums and differences, although she was able to demonstrate addition and subtraction both with manipulatives and on paper. Initially, she was not able to demonstrate the concept of division.

In one of our first sessions, Alicia was asked to use a rectangle to model multiplication. She needed assistance to remember what shape a rectangle was, but once she was taught, she routinely built rectangular arrays to model math facts. She understood the concept of multiplication best when she was asked to use concrete materials to make multiple groups of a number, and when she was asked to create arrays.

At first, she did not associate the multiplication facts with skip counting or with any conceptual link. Although she reported doing "fan math" (single- by multiple-digit multiplication) and "cowboy math" (double-digit multiplication), she did not appear to know the concept behind these processes.

On the Key Math Test, administered in August 2004, Alicia demonstrated understanding of basic math concepts at the 14th percentile (grade equivalent 4.3). Her understanding of geometry was a relative strength. She had difficulty with questions requiring her to round numbers and to read larger numbers. Similarly, she struggled to answer questions about fractions and decimals.

Language

Throughout the diagnostic teaching process, Alicia demonstrated incomplete understanding of math vocabulary. She required frequent repetition and practice to recall terms such as *array, rectangle, product, sum,* and *equivalent.* She benefited from keeping a strategy notebook, with a section designated for vocabulary.

Application

Alicia's ability to apply math concepts to everyday problems was inconsistent. On the Key Math Test, she demonstrated a relative strength in her understanding of time and money (37th percentile). However, she struggled to make the connection between mathematical operations and their application in real life. For example, she had difficulty determining the appropriate mathematical procedure needed to solve given problems. She also had trouble estimating quantities, and she overrelied on concrete operations rather than estimating to make sure her answer "made sense." On the Key Math Test, she scored at the 18th percentile (4.6 grade equivalent) on the Applications cluster, which measured her understanding of measurement, time and money, interpretation of data, problem solving, and estimation.

Procedures

Many of our educational therapy sessions were spent clarifying the connection between rote mathematical procedures that Alicia had learned and their mathematical meaning. Alicia relied on the strategies and methods that she had been taught to compute the answers to addition, subtraction, and multiplication problems. She correctly described the "fan math" procedure and "cowboy math" for solving double-digit multiplication problems. However, further exploration revealed that Alicia's understanding of the concepts behind these procedures was limited. When asked about some of these operations, she responded, "We did that already last year. We don't do that anymore." Her responses reflected a lack of understanding of the connection between mathematical procedures and a limited number sense. During educational therapy sessions, Alicia has benefited from a review of the four operations, their purposes, and key words that reflect the meaning of each operation. She will require more review to grasp these concepts fully.

On the Key Math Test, Alicia's performance on the Operations section represented a relative weakness. Overall, she performed at the 6th percentile when asked to compute addition, subtraction, multiplication, and division problems. She solved addition and subtraction problems more successfully than multiplication and division. She forgot to regroup on the subtraction problems, but when reminded, she corrected her answers. Several of her errors on the computation section of this test reflected her lack of attention to details and lack of automatic recall of math facts rather than a lack of understanding of the procedures.

Summary of Math Evaluation

Results of diagnostic educational therapy and formal testing indicated that although Alicia has learned procedures and operations for math calculations, she has not made a conceptual link between the operations and the concepts underlying them. Her lack of number sense has interfered with her ability to understand math concepts. Findings indicated that Alicia needs a math curriculum that proceeds slowly, in small units, with frequent spiral teaching to review previously learned concepts and link them to new information.

Goals of Educational Therapy

As a result of the initial diagnostic work with Alicia, the following goals were developed:

1. Help Alicia to link math operations to their underlying concepts.

2. Develop Alicia's number sense further through the use of concrete and semiconcrete strategies.
3. Build Alicia's automaticity of multiplication facts, while encouraging her to use a math chart and to develop strategies for the facts she has not automatized.
4. Help Alicia develop an understanding of fractions, including concepts, language, application, and procedures.

Summary of Educational Therapy

During the summer of 2004, Alicia worked primarily on multiplication facts. Each session included activities designed to link these facts to the concept of multiplication. Concrete materials were used to build arrays, and these were copied onto graph paper. Facts were addressed systematically. Alicia began to use a "key word" strategy to solve multiplication and division word problems.

In the fall, systematic communication with Alicia's teacher, Ms. Nickerson, enabled the educational therapy sessions to complement Alicia's curriculum at school. Alicia benefited from beginning a review of all mathematical operations. In addition, a major focus of the sessions has been on making a connection between division (like "dealing cards") and multiplying ("making more and more"). We continued to illustrate pencil-and-paper operations using foam squares or playing cards. We also addressed Alicia's difficulties with place value, using playing cards to build big numbers and read them.

Since winter break, we have been working on fractions and decimals. Alicia has made excellent use of concrete and visual representations that help her to understand these concepts. She has benefited from repeated instruction focused on the links between previously taught concepts and current ideas. For example, we spent one session linking fractions and decimals using three-column note taking. She continues to need frequent repetition and practice of earlier skills and strategies to retain them.

Alicia benefits from "recipes" and clear-cut procedures for math. She continues to need direct questioning and concrete demonstrations to make these procedures meaningful for her.

Recommendations

General Recommendations

1. Because Alicia's last evaluation is 3 years old, she could benefit from a new neuropsychological evaluation, which would clarify her profile of learning strengths and weaknesses.

2. Alicia's learning style suggests that she will benefit from a curriculum that moves slowly, in micro-units, from one concept to the next. The order of topics should proceed in logical fashion so that a new topic relies on the previously learned concept. One topic should be practiced until Alicia is very familiar with it and approaches mastery.

3. Because Alicia's processing speed is slow, she should not be expected to offer rapid responses on math tests. She should work toward automaticity by learning strategies for remembering or figuring out math facts.

4. To help Alicia maintain her high level of effort and persistence in math, she will need to be engaged frequently in tasks where she can experience success. She will respond to frequent positive reinforcement for her efforts.

5. Alicia may need an alternative to the traditional Massachusetts Comprehensive Assessment System (MCAS). The possibility of a portfolio assessment should be discussed by her team at Pine School. If Alicia has to take the traditional MCAS, then she will need several accommodations, including permission to use a calculator for the entire math portion of the test. These accommodations should be discussed and appropriate ones should be decided upon at a team meeting of her teachers and parents.

Specific Instructional Recommendations

6. Each of Alicia's math lessons should address the following areas:
   a. Concepts
   b. Math language
   c. Procedures
   d. Application

7. Alicia would benefit from keeping a strategy notebook at school and another for use in tutoring sessions. These notebooks could have one section devoted to vocabulary and another for strategies that have helped Alicia learn math facts or concepts. The bulk of the notebook could be notes and examples from her class. A three-column format, including a term in one column, a diagram in the next, and a mathematical example in the third, may help Alicia organize mathematical information in her mind.

8. To learn her math facts, Alicia would benefit from a multisensory and strategic approach. She should put a few known facts on index cards, kept together on a ring. On the front of a card, she should write the problem, and on the back, she should record a strategy that she could use to remember the answer. This could be anything that helps her remember the answer, such as a diagram using pictures of manipulative

materials, a word problem, a rhyme, or a close-by fact (e.g., to remember 7 × 6, think "I know 7 × 5," then add 1 more 7). She should review these facts every day, and no new facts should be added until she knows the ones already on the ring.

9. Simultaneously with learning the multiplication facts, Alicia should be taught to use "friendly" numbers (multiples of 10 and 100) to solve problems.

10. Whenever the object of the lesson is to focus on developing a math *concept,* Alicia should be allowed to use a calculator for the computation. She should be systematically taught how to use a calculator to compute.

11. Alicia would benefit from a step-by-step strategy for word problems that involves underlining important parts of the question, circling the numbers, paraphrasing the question, choosing an operation, writing a number sentence, solving, and checking.

12. Alicia would benefit from direct instruction in real-life applications of math, including money, time, and measurement.

13. As much as possible, Alicia's math instruction should proceed from concrete to semiconcrete to abstract, to enhance her ability to understand the underlying concepts.

14. Alicia clearly benefits from using visual representations of math concepts. She should record information in her notebook using diagrams and color coding, which will aid her retention.

I have enjoyed getting to know Alicia. She is a delightful student and a hard worker.

Sincerely,

Joan Steinberg, MEd

Appendix B

Reproducible Materials

Venn Diagram for Comparison/Contrast

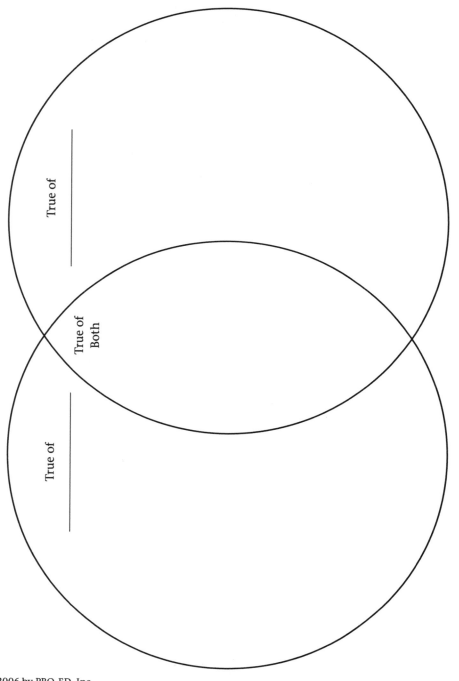

True of

True of
Both

True of

Star Strategy

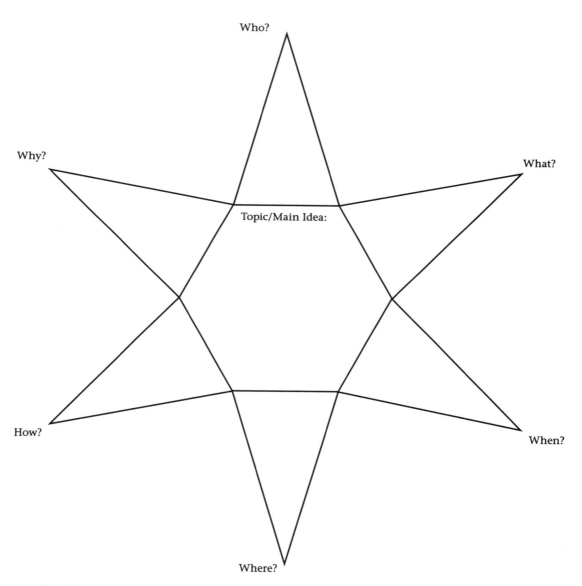

Who?

Why?

What?

Topic/Main Idea:

How?

When?

Where?

Note. The Star strategy is a prewriting organizer developed by S. Taber, Institute for Learning and Development, Lexington, MA.

Appendix B.3

Pieces of a Thesis

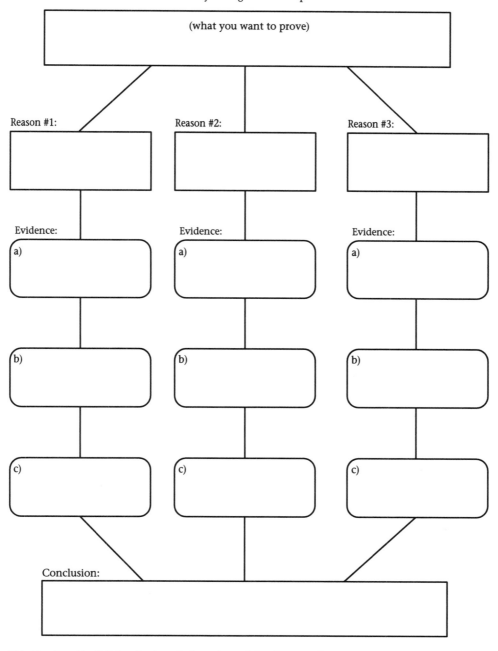

State your argument or topic:

(what you want to prove)

Reason #1:

Reason #2:

Reason #3:

Evidence:

a)

b)

c)

Evidence:

a)

b)

c)

Evidence:

a)

b)

c)

Conclusion:

Note. Developed by S. Taber, Institute for Learning and Development, Lexington, MA.

Transition Words (Examples)

Time Sequences

first	eventually	next
then	so far	afterward
later	at the same time	after all
earlier	in the meantime	finally
soon		

Spatial Order

behind	in front of	outside
farther on	ahead of	next to
inside	together	to the left

Order of Importance

most important	for this reason	second
after all	in reality	third
furthermore	consequently	as a matter of fact
also	in addition	for this reason

Contrast

however	on the other hand	but
in contrast	on the contrary	although
while	nevertheless	

Concluding

as you can see	in conclusion
finally	in summary

Learning Profile Venn

Student _____

Date _____ Teacher _____

Strengths

Areas of Difficulty

Average or
Inconsistent

Recommendations

Appendix B.6

Learning Style Student Survey

Name _____ Date _____

Check the answer that best expresses your learning style:

	Yes	Sometimes	No
1. I wonder about things and like to find out about them.	☐	☐	☐
2. I like to share my ideas by talking.	☐	☐	☐
3. I like to share my ideas by using dialogue.	☐	☐	☐
4. I like to share my ideas by drawing.	☐	☐	☐
5. I like to share my ideas by writing.	☐	☐	☐
6. I am persistent with things that seem hard.	☐	☐	☐
7. When something is difficult, I need to take more time.	☐	☐	☐
8. When writing a paper, it's hard to get started.	☐	☐	☐
9. I like my work space to be neat and organized.	☐	☐	☐
10. I like to make pictures in my head when reading.	☐	☐	☐

Complete the following sentences:

I organize my books and materials by _____

_____

_____

It is easier for me to remember things by (hearing, seeing, doing, etc.) _____

_____

_____

In order for me to concentrate, I need _____

_____

_____

Note. Adapted from Pike School, Andover, MA.

Examine Your Teaching Style

There are four basic learning modalities:

1. Visual (seen)
2. Auditory (heard)
3. Kinesthetic (movement)
4. Tactile (touch)

When you are teaching, it is helpful to stay aware of how you are imparting information to the whole class. Often, teachers unconsciously convey information according to their own learning styles. However, it is important to keep in mind that the room is filled with diverse learners, many of whom prefer a multisensory approach, or a combination of learning modalities.

Take the following quiz by checking the most appropriate answer according to how you would react most often.

1. You usually remember more from a lecture by
   ☐ a. listening carefully.
   ☐ b. watching the speaker or reading the overhead slides.
   ☐ c. taking lots of notes even if you'll never use them again.

2. You usually solve problems by
   ☐ a. talking to yourself or a friend.
   ☐ b. using an organized, systematic approach with lists, schedules, etc.
   ☐ c. walking, pacing, or some other physical activity.

3. You remember phone numbers (when you can't write them down) by
   ☐ a. repeating the numbers orally.
   ☐ b. "seeing" or "visualizing" the numbers in your mind.
   ☐ c. "writing" the numbers with your finger on a table or wall.

4. You find it easiest to learn something new by
   - ☐ a. listening to someone explain how to do it.
   - ☐ b. watching a demonstration of how to do it.
   - ☐ c. trying it yourself.

5. You remember parts from a movie most clearly by
   - ☐ a. what the characters said, background noises, and music.
   - ☐ b. the setting, scenery, and costumes.
   - ☐ c. the feelings you experienced during the movie.

6. When you go to the supermarket, you
   - ☐ a. silently or orally repeat the grocery list to yourself.
   - ☐ b. walk up and down the aisles to see what you need.
   - ☐ c. usually remember what you need from the list you left at home.

7. When you are trying to remember something, you
   - ☐ a. hear in your mind what was said or the noises that occurred.
   - ☐ b. try to see it happen in your mind.
   - ☐ c. feel the way "it" reacted with your emotions.

8. You learn a foreign language best by
   - ☐ a. listening to audiocassettes or CDs and repeating back.
   - ☐ b. writing in and reviewing workbooks.
   - ☐ c. attending a class in which you read and write.

9. When you are confused about the correct spelling of a word, you
   - ☐ a. sound it out.
   - ☐ b. try to "see" the word in your mind.
   - ☐ c. write the word several different ways and choose the one that looks right.

10. You enjoy reading most when you can read
    - ☐ a. dialogue between characters.
    - ☐ b. descriptive passages that allow you to create mental pictures.
    - ☐ c. stories with a lot of action in the beginning (because you have a hard time sitting still).

11. You usually remember people you have met by their
    ☐   a. names (you forget faces).
    ☐   b. faces (you forget names).
    ☐   c. mannerisms, motions, etc.

12. You are distracted most by
    ☐   a. noises.
    ☐   b. people.
    ☐   c. environment (temperature, comfort of furniture, etc.).

13. You usually dress
    ☐   a. fairly well (but clothes are not very important to you).
    ☐   b. neatly (in a particular style).
    ☐   c. comfortably (so you can move easily).

14. If you couldn't do anything physical and couldn't read, you would choose to
    ☐   a. talk with a friend.
    ☐   b. watch TV or look out a window.
    ☐   c. move slightly in your chair or bed.

SCORING

1. Count the total number of responses for each letter and write them below:

   a. _____   auditory   (learn best by hearing)
   b. _____   visual   (learn best by seeing)
   c. _____   kinesthetic   (learn best by touching, doing, moving)

2. Notice if one modality is significantly higher or lower, or if any two modalities are close in number.

3. Were the results as you expected them to be? Are your preferred learning style and teaching style the same?

Note. Adapted from Incentive Publications, Inc., Nashville, TN.

Appendix C

Recommended Resources

Resources About Learning Disabilities and Attention-Deficit/Hyperactivity Disorder

Barkley, R. (1995). *Taking charge of ADHD.* New York: Guilford Press.

Cicci, R. (1995). *What's wrong with me? Learning disabilities at home and school.* Baltimore: York Press.

Goldstein, S., & Mather, N. (1998). *Overcoming underachieving: An action guide to helping your child succeed in school.* Hoboken, NJ: Wiley.

Hallowell, E., & Ratey, J. (1994). *Driven to distraction: Recognizing and coping with ADD, from childhood through adulthood.* New York: Pantheon Books.

Levine, M. (1994). *Educational care: A system for understanding and helping children with learning problems at home and in school.* Cambridge, MA: Educators Publishing Service.

Levine, M. (1995). *A mind at a time.* New York: Simon & Schuster.

Mastropieri, M. A., & Scruggs, T. E. (2003). *The inclusive classroom: Strategies for effective instruction* (2nd ed.). Upper Saddle River, NJ: Prentice Hall.

Meltzer, L., Roditi, B., & Stein, J. (1998, Summer). Strategy instruction: The heartbeat of successful inclusion. *Perspectives, 24*(3), 10–13.

Meltzer, L., Roditi, B., & Stein, J. (2002, January). Can we help all children succeed? Preserving process learning in the era of high stakes testing: Research-based strategies for teaching and test taking. *Perspectives,* 10–12.

Meltzer, L. T., Roditi, B., Stein, J., Krishna, K., & Pollica, L. (2004). *Effective study and test-taking strategies for kids with learning difficulties.* Available online from www.schwablearning.org

Nadeau, K., Littman, E., & Quinn, P. (1999). *Understanding girls with AD/HD.* Silver Spring, MD: Advantage Books.

Oliver, C., & Bowler, R. F. (1996). *Learning to learn.* New York: Fireside Press.

Pressley, M., & Harris, K. (1990, September). What we really know about strategy instruction. *Educational Leadership,* 31–34.

Rief, S. E. (1998). *The ADD/ADHD checklist.* New York: Prentice Hall Trade.

Sanders, M. (2000). *Understanding dyslexia and the reading process: A guide for educators and parents.* Boston: Allyn & Bacon.

Siegel, L. M. (2001). *The complete IEP guide: How to advocate for your special ed child.* Berkeley, CA: Nolo Press.

Silver, L. B. (1998). *The misunderstood child: Understanding and coping with your child's learning disabilities* (3rd ed.). New York: Three Rivers Press.

Smith, S. (1999). *No easy answers: The learning disabled child at home and at school.* New York: Bantam Books.

Stein, J., Meltzer, L., Krishna, K., Sales-Pollica, L., Papadopoulos, I., & Roditi, B. (in press). *Making homework work at home.* New York: Scholastic.

WGBH Educational Foundation and All Kinds of Minds (Producer). (2002). *Developing minds* [Video]. (Available from http://www.wgbh.org)

Resources About the Social and Emotional Aspects of Learning Differences

Brooks, B. (1991). *The self-esteem teacher.* Circle Pines, MN: American Guidance Service.

Brooks, B. (Director), & Public Broadcasting System (Producer). (1997). *Look what you've done! Stories of hope and resilience for parents and teachers* [Video]. (Available from http://www.drrobertbrooks.com)

Brooks, B., & Goldstein, S. (2001). *Raising resilient children: Fostering strength, hope and optimism in your child.* Chicago: McGraw-Hill Contemporary Books.

Hallowell, E. M. (1997). *When you worry about the child you love.* New York: Fireside Press.

Hallowell, E. M. (1998). *CONNECT: 12 vital ties that open your heart, lengthen your life, and deepen your soul.* New York: Pantheon Books.

Osman, B. (1995). *No one to play with: The social problems of LD and ADD children.* Novato, CA: Academic Therapy Press.

Osman, B. (1997). *Learning disabilities and ADHD: A family guide to living and learning together.* Indianapolis, IN: Wiley.

Ryan, M. (1994). *Social and emotional problems of dyslexia: The other sixteen hours* (Orton Emeritus Series Book). Baltimore: International Dyslexia Association.

Resources About Nonverbal Learning Disabilities

Rourke, B. (1995). *Syndrome of nonverbal learning disabilities: Neurodevelopmental manifestations.* New York: Guilford Press.

Stewart, K. (2002). *Helping a child with nonverbal learning disorder or Asperger's syndrome: A parent's guide.* Oakland, CA: New Harbinger.

Tanguay, P. B. (2001). *Nonverbal learning disabilities at home: A parent's guide.* Cambridge, MA: Athenaeum Press.

Thompson, S. (1997). *The source for nonverbal learning disorders.* Chicago Heights, IL: Linguisystems.

Varney, R. V. (2002). *Bridging the gap: Raising a child with nonverbal learning disorder.* New York: Perigee.

Books for Teens About Learning Disabilities and Attention-Deficit/Hyperactivity Disorder

Cobb, J. (2001). *Learning how to learn: Getting into and surviving college when you have a learning disability.* Washington, DC: Child Welfare League of America.

Cummings, R., & Fisher, G. (1993). *School survival guide for teenagers with LD.* Minneapolis: Free Spirit.

Mooney, J., & Cole, D. (2000). *Learning outside the lines: Two Ivy League students with learning disabilities and ADHD give you the tools for academic success and educational revolution.* New York: Simon & Schuster.

Nadeau, K. (1994). *Survival guide for college students with ADD or LD*. Washington, DC: Magination Press.

Nadeau, K. (1998). *Help4ADD@HighSchool*. Silver Spring, MD: Advantage Books.

Porterfield, K. M. (1999). *Straight talk about learning disabilities*. New York: Facts on File.

Reif, S. F. (1993). *How to reach and teach ADD children*. West Nyack, NY: Center for Applied Research In Education.

Willens, T. (1998). *Straight talk about psychiatric medications for kids*. New York: Guilford Press.

Books for Children About Learning Disabilities and Attention-Deficit/Hyperactivity Disorder

Betancourt, J. (1993). *My name is Brain/Brian*. New York: Scholastic.

Fisher, G. L., & Cummings, R. E. (2002). *The school survival guide for kids with LD (learning differences)*. Minneapolis: Free Spirit.

Gehret, J. (1990). *The don't give up kid and learning differences*. Fairport, NY: Verbal Images Press.

Lauren, J. (1997). *Succeeding with LD: 20 true stories about real people with LD*. Minneapolis: Free Spirit.

Levine, M. (1990). *Keeping a head in school*. Cambridge, MA: Educators Publishing Service.

Levine, M. (1997). *All kinds of minds*. Cambridge, MA: Educators Publishing Service.

Schlieper, A. (1995). *The best fight*. Morton Grove, IL: Albert Whitman.

Resources About Strategies and Instruction in Specific Areas

Reading and Writing

Bley, N. S., & Thornton, C. A. (1989). *Teaching mathematics to the learning disabled*. Austin, TX: PRO-ED.

Clark, D. B. (1988). *Dyslexia: Theory and practice of remedial instruction*. Parkton, MD: York.

Collins, J. (1992). *Developing writing and thinking skills across the curriculum: A practical program for schools*. West Newberry, MA: Collins Education Associates.

Curtis, M. E., & Longo, A. M. (1999). *When adolescents can't read: Methods and materials that work*. Cambridge, MA: Brookline Books.

Dupuis, M. M. (Ed.). (1984). *Reading in the content areas: Research for teachers*. Newark, DE: International Reading Association.

Garner, R. (1987). *Metacognition and reading comprehension*. Norwood, NJ: Ablex.

Harris, K., & Graham, S. (1999). *Making the writing process work: Strategies for composition and self-regulation (Cognitive Strategy Training)*. Cambridge, MA: Brookline Books.

Jennings, T. M., & Haynes, C. W. (2002). *From talking to writing: Strategies for scaffolding expository expression*. Beverly Farms, MA: Landmark School Inc. and Terrill M. Jennings and Charles W. Haynes.

ResearchILD and FableVision (Producers). (2005). Essay express [Computer software]. (Available from http://www.fablevision.com)

Tarricone, J. G. (1995). *Writing: A Landmark School teaching guide.* Beverly Farms, MA: Landmark School Inc. and Jean Gudaitis Tarricone.

Study and Test-Taking Strategies

Institute for Learning and Development/ResearchILD and FableVision (Producers). (2001). *BrainCogs: The test taking survival kit* [Computer software]. (Available from http://www.braincogs.com)

Sedita, J. (2002). *Study skills: A Landmark School teaching guide* (2nd ed.). Beverly Farms, MA: Landmark School Inc. and Joan Sedita.

Math

Carnine, D. (1997). Instructional design in math for students with learning disabilities. *Journal of Learning Disabilities, 30,* 142–150.

Carpenter, T., & Fennema, E. (1999). *Children's mathematics: Cognitively guided instruction.* Portsmouth, NH: Heinemann.

Cognition and Technology Group at Vanderbilt University. (1997). *The Jasper Project: Lessons in curriculum, instruction, assessment and professional development.* Mahwah, NJ: Erlbaum.

Hiebert, J., Carpenter, T., Fennema, E., Fuson, K., et al. (1997). *Making sense: Teaching and learning mathematics with understanding.* Portsmouth, NH: Heinemann.

Montague, M. (1985). Teaching verbal mathematical problem solving skills to students. In C. Simon (Ed.), *Communication skills and classroom success: Therapy methodologies for language-learning disabled students* (pp. 365–377). San Diego, CA: College-Hill.

National Council of Teachers of Mathematics. (1999). *Principles and standards of mathematics 2000.* Reston, VA: National Council of Teachers of Mathematics.

Northwest Regional Educational Laboratory. (1998). *Improving classroom assessment: A toolkit for professional developers.* Portland, OR: Author.

Russell, S. J. (2000). Developing computational fluency with whole numbers in the elementary grades. *New England Mathematics Journal, 32*(2), 40–54.

Semple, J. L. (n.d.). *Semple Math.* Attleboro Falls, MA: Stevenson Learning Skills. (Available from http://www.stevensonsemple.com)

Sharma, M. (1990, September–December issues). Dyslexia, dyscalculia, and some remedial perspectives for mathematics learning problems. *Math Notebook: From Theory into Practice, 8*(7–10).

Sharma, M. (n.d.). *Six levels of knowing math notebooks.* Framingham, MA: Center for Teaching and Learning of Mathematics.

TouchMath. (n.d.). Colorado Springs, CO: Innovative Learning Concepts. (Available at http://www.touchmath.com)

Woodin, C. (1995). *The Landmark method for teaching arithmetic.* Beverly Farms, MA: Landmark School Inc. and Christopher Woodin. (Available from http://www.landmarkschool.org)

Math Software

Algebra Class (William K. Bradford Publishing Company)

Carmen Sandiego Math Detective (The Learning Company)

Logical Journey of the Zoombinis (Broderbund)

Math Pad and Math Pad Plus (Intellitools)

Number Maze Challenge (Great Wave Software)
Numbers Undercover (Sunburst Publications)
Spending Money (Attainment Company)
Treasure Math Storms (Edmark)

Web Resources

Asperger Syndrome Coalition of the U.S. (http://www.maapservices.org)—Run by a nonprofit association dedicated to providing current, comprehensive information on Asperger syndrome; provides an extensive collection of articles on the topic, support group listings, and resources.

Attention Deficit Disorder Association (http://www.add.org)—Offers information on a collection of topics including career challenges; includes section for kids and teens.

FableVision (http://www.fablevision.com)—Experts in creating imaginative technological tools that are reflective of diverse pathways to learning. Collaborators with Institute for Learning and Development and ResearchILD in producing BrainCogs and Essay Express.

International Dyslexia Association (http://www.interdys.org)—Provides information about dyslexia sorted by audience (teens, college students, parents, educators, and adults); offers articles and items for purchase.

LD Online (http://www.ldonline.org)—Colorful and easily maneuvered site offers great basic information on learning disabilities plus active updates of an events calendar; includes sections for teachers and children as well as parents; great all-purpose site.

National Center for Learning Disabilities (http://www.ncld.org)—This national organization provides information, resources, and referral services for parents, adults, and teens with learning disabilities; also reviews laws and opportunities for advocacy.

NLD on the Web (http://www.nldontheweb.org)—Contains a well-organized collection of articles and resources.

ResearchILD (www.researchild.org)—A well-designed site by a nonprofit organization dedicated to cutting-edge research and dissemination of information about learning disabilities.

Schwab Learning (http://www.Schwablearning.org)—A well-designed site by a nonprofit association dedicated to helping parents of children with learning disabilities; very clear and easy to get around; also in Spanish.

Math Web Resources

http://www.pbskids.org/cyberchase (problems that come from the TV series)
http://www.multiplication.com/interactive_games.htm
http://www.k111.k12.il.us/king/math.htm (interactive games)
http://www.shodor.org/interactivate/activities (interesting interactive activities for all levels)

http://coe.jmu.edu/mathvidsr (highly recommended site with strategies for teaching math to students who have difficulty learning math)

http://matti.usu.edu/nlvm/nav/topic_t_2.html (National Library of Virtual Manipulatives)

http://www.bbc.co.uk/education/mathsfile/gameswheel.html (clever games from Britain, complete with ridiculous, printable prizes; also accessible through http://www.nldontheweb.org—go to Interventions and follow the links to math games and activities)

http://www.exemplars.com (sample performance-based assessment problems with rubrics)

Web Sites for Publishers of Materials for Students with Learning Disabilities

ENC Eisenhower National Clearinghouse, U.S. Department of Education: http://www.enc.org

FableVision: http://www.fablevision.com

Glencoe: http://www.glencoe.com

Harcourt: http://www.harcourt.com

Houghton Mifflin: http://www.hmco.com/indexf.html

Prentice Hall: http://vig.prenhall.com

PRO-ED: http://www.proedinc.com

Remedia: http://www.rempub.com/stores

http://www.funbrain.com (activities for basic facts)

http://www.digi-block.com (manipulatives for students)

References

Adams, M. J. (1990). *Beginning to read: Thinking and learning about print.* Cambridge, MA: MIT Press.

Atwell, N. (1987). *In the middle: Writing, reading, and learning with adolescents.* Portsmouth, NH: Heinemann.

Bell, N. (1991a). *Visualizing and verbalizing.* San Luis Obispo, CA: Gander.

Bell, N. (1991b). *Visualizing and verbalizing: For language comprehension and thinking.* Paso Robles, CA: Academy of Reading.

Bell, N. (1997). *Seeing stars.* San Luis Obispo, CA: Gander.

Bloom, B. S. (Ed.). (1956). *Taxonomy of educational objectives: The classification of educational goals: Handbook I, cognitive domain.* New York: Longmans, Green.

Brooks, R. (1991). *The self-esteem teacher.* Circle Pines, MN: American Guidance Service.

Brown, A. L., & Campione, J. C. (1986). Psychological theory and the study of learning disabilities. *American Psychologist, 41,* 1059–1068.

Butler, A. (1988). *Guided reading.* Crystal Lake, IL: Rigby.

Byars, B. (1989). *Trouble River.* New York: Puffin Books. (Originally published 1969)

Campbell, K. (1998). *Great Leaps Reading.* Gainesville, FL: Diarmuid.

Chall, J. S. (1987). Two vocabularies for reading: Recognition and meaning. In M. G. McKeown & M. E. Curtis (Eds.), *The nature of vocabulary acquisition* (pp. 7–17). Hillsdale, NJ: Erlbaum.

Chase, A., & Duffelmeyer, F. (1990). VOCAB–LIT: Integrating vocabulary study and literature study. *Journal of Reading, 34,* 188–193.

Ciborowski, J. (1992). *Textbooks and the student who can't read them.* Cambridge, MA: Brookline Books.

Coburn, T. G., Hoogeboom, S., & Goodnow, J. (1989). *The problem solver with calculators.* Mountain View, CA: Creative Publications.

Collins, J. (1992). *Developing writing and thinking skills across the curriculum: A practical program for schools.* West Newbury, MA: Collins Education Associates.

Curtis, M. E. (1986). The best kind of vocabulary instruction. *Massachusetts Primer, 15,* 5–9.

Curtis, M. E. (1987). Vocabulary testing and vocabulary instruction. In M. G. McKeown & M. E. Curtis (Eds.), *The nature of vocabulary acquisition* (pp. 37–51). Hillsdale, NJ: Erlbaum.

Denckla, M. D., & Rudel, R. G. (1976). Rapid Automatized Naming (RAN) differentiated from other learning disabilities. *Neuropsychologia, 14,* 471–479.

Deshler, D. D., & Schumaker, J. B. (1986). Learning strategies: An instructional alternative for low achieving adolescents. *Exceptional Children, 52,* 583–590.

Donnelly, K., Miller, L., & Wolf, M. (2000). Retrieval, Automaticity, Vocabulary Elaboration, Orthography (RAVE-O): A comprehensive, fluency-based reading intervention program. *Journal of Learning Disabilities, 33*(4), 375–386.

Fry, E. B., Kress, J. E., & Fountoukidis, D. C. (2000). *The reading teacher's book of lists* (2nd ed.). Paramus, NJ: Prentice Hall.

Fuchs, L. S., & Fuchs, D. (2002). Curriculum-based measurement: Describing competence, enhancing outcomes, evaluating treatment effects, and identifying treatment nonresponders. *Peabody Journal of Education, 77,* 64–84.

Graham, L., & Wong, B. (1993). Comparing two modes of teaching a question-answering strategy for enhancing reading comprehension: Didactic and self-instruction training. *Journal of Learning Disabilities, 26,* 270–279.

Greene, V., & Enfield, M. (1999). *Project Read: Phonology guide, Framing your thoughts, Story form, Report form.* Bloomington, MN: Language Circle Enterprises.

Greenes, C., Immerzerl, G., Schulman, L., & Spungin, R. (1989). *TOPS calculator problem deck IV.* Palo Alto, CA: Dale Seymour.

Harris, K., & Graham, S. (1992). *Helping young writers master the craft: Strategy instruction and self-regulation in the writing process.* Cambridge, MA: Brookline Books.

Harris, K. R., & Graham, S. (1996). *Making the writing process work: Strategies for composition and self-regulation.* Cambridge, MA: Brookline Books.

Harris, K. R., Graham, S., & Mason, L. (2002). POW plus TREE equals powerful opinion essays. *Teaching Exceptional Children, 34,* 74–77.

Harrison, D. (1972). *The book of giant stories.* New York: American Heritage Press.

Hasselbring, T., Goin, L., & Bransford, J. (1988). Developing math automaticity in learning handicapped children: The role of computerized drill and practice. *Teaching Exceptional Children, 20*(6), 3–7.

Hillocks, G. (1986). *Research on written composition: New directions for teaching.* Urbana, IL: Clearinghouse on Reading and Communication Skills and the National Conference on Research in English.

Ihnot, C. (1991). *Read naturally.* St. Paul, MN: Read Naturally.

Indrisano, R. (1984). Reading and writing revisited. *Ginn Occasional Papers.* Columbus, OH: Ginn.

Institute for Learning and Development/ResearchILD and FableVision (2001). Brain-Cogs: The test taking survival kit [Computer software]. (Available from http://www.fablevision.com/braincogs)

Jennings, T. M., & Haynes, C. W. (2002). *From talking to writing: Strategies for scaffolding expository expression.* Beverly Farms, MA: Landmark School Inc. and Terrill M. Jennings and Charles W. Haynes.

Licht, B. (1993). Achievement-related beliefs in children with learning disabilities: Impact on motivation and strategic learning. In L. J. Meltzer (Ed.), *Strategy assessment and instruction for students with learning disabilities: From theory to practice* (pp. 195–220). Austin, TX: PRO-ED.

Lindamood, P., & Lindamood, P. (1998). *The Lindamood phoneme sequencing program for reading, spelling, and speech.* Austin, TX: PRO-ED.

Mastropieri, M., Scruggs, T., & Levin, J. (1985). Maximizing what exceptional children can learn: A review of research on the keyword method and related mnemonic techniques. *Remedial and Special Education, 6*(2), 39–45.

Meltzer, L. J. (1993a). Assessment of learning disabilities: The challenge of evaluating the cognitive strategies and processes underlying learning. In G. R. Lyon (Ed.), *Frames of reference for the assessment of learning disabilities* (pp. 571–606). Baltimore: Brookes.

Meltzer, L. J. (1993b). Strategy use in children with learning disabilities: The challenge of assessment. In L. J. Meltzer (Ed.), *Strategy assessment and instruction for students with learning disabilities: From theory to practice* (pp. 93–136). Austin, TX: PRO-ED.

Meltzer, L. J. (1996). Strategic learning in LD students: The role of students' self-awareness and self-perceptions. In T. Scruggs & M. Mastropieri (Eds.), *Advances in learning and behavioral disabilities* (pp. 181–199). Greenwich, CT: JAI Press.

REFERENCES223

Meltzer, L. J. (2004). Resilience and learning disabilities: The search for internal and external protective dynamics. *Learning Disabilities Research and Practice, 19*(1), 1–2.

Meltzer, L. J., Houser, R., Perlman, M., & Roditi, B. (1998). Perceptions of academic strategies and competence in students with learning disabilities. *Journal of Learning Disabilities, 31,* 437–451.

Meltzer, L., Katzir, T., Miller, L., Reddy, R., & Roditi, B. (2004). Academic self-perceptions, effort, and strategy use in students with learning disabilities: Changes over time. *Learning Disabilities Research & Practice, 19*(2), 99–108.

Meltzer, L. J., Katzir-Cohen, T., Miller, L., & Roditi, B. (2001). The impact of effort and strategy use on academic performance: Student and teacher perceptions. *Learning Disabilities Quarterly, 24*(2), 85–98.

Meltzer, L. J., & Montague, M. (2001). Strategic learning in students with learning disabilities: What have we learned? In D. Hallahan & B. K. Keogh (Eds.), *Research and global perspectives in learning disabilities: Essays in honor of William J. Cruickshank* (pp. 111–130). Hillsdale, NJ: Erlbaum.

Meltzer, L., Reddy, R., Pollica, L. S., & Roditi, B. (2004, Fall). Academic success in students with learning disabilities: The roles of self-understanding, strategy use, and effort. In *Thalamus—Journal of the International Academy for Research in Learning Disabilities, 22*(1), 16–32.

Meltzer, L. J., Reddy, R., Pollica, L. S., Roditi, B., Sayer, J., & Theokas, C. (2004). Positive and negative self-perceptions: Is there a cyclical relationship between teachers' and students' perceptions of effort, strategy use and academic performance? *Learning Disabilities Research and Practice, 19*(1), 33–34.

Meltzer, L., Roditi, B., & Stein, J. (1998, Summer). Strategy instruction: The heartbeat of successful inclusion. *Perspectives, 24*(3), 10–13.

Meltzer, L., Roditi, B., & Stein, J. (2002, January). Can we help all children succeed? Preserving process learning in the era of high stakes testing: Research-based strategies for teaching and test taking. *Perspectives,* 10–12.

Meltzer, L. T., Roditi, B., Stein, J., Krishna, K., & Pollica, L. (2004). *Effective study and test-taking strategies for kids with learning difficulties.* Retrieved May 27, 2005, from www.schwablearning.org

Mercer, C. D., & Campbell, K. U. (1998). *Great Leaps Reading K–2.* Gainesville, FL: Diarmuid.

Miller, S. P., & Mercer, C. D. (1993). Mnemonics: Enhancing the math performance of students with learning difficulties. *Intervention in School and Clinic, 29*(2), 78–82.

Moreau, M. E. R., & Fidrych-Puzzo, H. (2002). *How to use the story grammar marker.* Springfield, MA: MindWing Concepts.

Nagy, W., Herman, P., & Anderson, R. (1985). Learning words from context. *Reading Research Quarterly, 20,* 233–253.

National Council of Teachers of Mathematics. (2000). Principles and standards. Retrieved January 22, 2005, from http://www.nctm.org

Orton, J. (1966). The Orton–Gillingham approach. In J. Money (Ed.), *The disabled reader: Education of the dyslexic child* (pp. 119–146). Baltimore: Johns Hopkins Press.

Pressley, M., Goodchild, F., Fleet, J., Zajchowski, R., & Evans, E. D. (1989). The challenges of classroom strategy instruction. *Elementary School Journal, 89,* 301–342.

Putnam, M. L., Deshler, D. D., & Schumaker, J. B. (1993). The investigation of setting demands: A missing link in learning strategy instruction. In L. Meltzer (Ed.), *Strategy assessment and instruction for students with learning disabilities: From theory to practice* (pp. 325–353). Austin, TX: PRO-ED.

ResearchILD and FableVision. (2005). Essay Express. [Computer software]. (Available from http://www.fablevision.com)

Rhodes, L. K., & Dudley-Marling, C. (1988). *Readers and writers with a difference.* Portsmouth, NH: Heinemann.

Roditi, B. (1993). Mathematics assessment and strategy instruction: An applied developmental approach. In L. J. Meltzer (Ed.), *Strategy assessment and instruction for students with learning disabilities: From theory to practice* (pp. 293–324). Austin, TX: PRO-ED.

Roswell, F. G., & Natchez, G. (1977). *Reading disability.* New York: Basic Books.

Sachar, L. (1989). *Wayside School is falling down.* New York: Avon.

Schroeder, M. A., & Washington, M. (1989). *Math in bloom.* East Moline, IL: LinguiSystems.

Sharma, M. (1989). *How children learn mathematics: Professor Mahesh Sharma, in interview with Bill Domoney.* [Videocassette]. London, England: Oxford Polytechnic, School of Education.

Squire, J. (1984). Composing and comprehending: Two sides of the same basic process. In J. M. Jensen (Ed.), *Composing and comprehending* (pp. 23–30). Urbana, IL: National Council of Teachers of English.

Stanovich, K. (1986). Matthew effects in reading: Some consequences of individual differences in the acquisition of literacy. *Reading Research Quarterly, 21,* 360–407.

Stein, J., Meltzer, L., Krishna, K., Sales-Pollica, L., Papadopoulos, I., & Roditi, B. (in press). *Making homework work at home.* New York: Scholastic.

Swanson, H. L., Hoskyn, M., & Lee, C. L. (1999). *Interventions for students with learning disabilities: A meta-analysis of treatment outcomes.* New York: Guilford Press.

Tarricone, J. G. (1995). *Writing: A Landmark School teaching guide.* Beverly Farms, MA: Landmark School and Jean Gudaitis Tarricone.

Wagner, R., Torgesen, J., & Rashotte, C. (1999). *Comprehensive Test of Phonological Processing.* Austin, TX: PRO-ED.

West, T. G. (1997). *In the mind's eye: visual thinkers, gifted people with dyslexia and other learning difficulties, computer images, and the ironies of creativity.* Amherst, NY: Prometheus Books.

Wilson, B. (1988). *Wilson reading system.* Millbury, MA: Wilson Language Training.

Wolf, M., & Denckla, M. B. (2005). *Rapid Automatized Naming and Rapid Alternating Stimulus Tests.* Austin, TX: PRO-ED.